Bernard Shaw and His Contemporaries

Series Editors
Nelson O'Ceallaigh Ritschel, Massachusetts Maritime Academy, Pocasset, MA, USA
Peter Gahan, Independent Scholar, Los Angeles, CA, USA

The series *Bernard Shaw and His Contemporaries* presents the best and most up-to-date research on Shaw and his contemporaries in a diverse range of cultural contexts. Volumes in the series will further the academic understanding of Bernard Shaw and those who worked with him, or in reaction against him, during his long career from the 1880s to 1950 as a leading writer in Britain and Ireland, and with a wide European and American following.

Shaw defined the modern literary theatre in the wake of Ibsen as a vehicle for social change, while authoring a dramatic canon to rival Shakespeare's. His careers as critic, essayist, playwright, journalist, lecturer, socialist, feminist, and pamphleteer, both helped to shape the modern world as well as pointed the way towards modernism. No one engaged with his contemporaries more than Shaw, whether as controversialist, or in his support of other, often younger writers. In many respects, therefore, the series as it develops will offer a survey of the rise of the modern at the beginning of the twentieth century and the subsequent varied cultural movements covered by the term modernism that arose in the wake of World War 1.

More information about this series at
https://link.springer.com/bookseries/14785

Bernard F. Dukore

Unions, Strikes, Shaw

"The Capitalism of the Proletariat"

palgrave
macmillan

Bernard F. Dukore
Virginia Tech
Blacksburg, VA, USA

ISSN 2634-5811 ISSN 2634-582X (electronic)
Bernard Shaw and His Contemporaries
ISBN 978-3-030-99130-2 ISBN 978-3-030-99131-9 (eBook)
https://doi.org/10.1007/978-3-030-99131-9

Cover credit: British General Strike of 1926: The Miners' Union, its funds dwindling, appeals to the public for donations for strikers

This Palgrave Macmillan imprint is published by the registered company Springer Nature Switzerland AG
The registered company address is: Gewerbestrasse 11, 6330 Cham, Switzerland

To DAN LAURENCE,
whose encouragement and advice,
early on and in many years to come,
were crucial and remain greatly appreciated

Acknowledgments

I am delighted to express my gratitude to my colleagues Michel Pharand, Nelson O'Ceallaigh Ritschel, and Peter Gahan. They exemplify the adage attributed to people as diverse as Benjamin Franklin and Lucille Ball (it's likely that both of them said it): if you want something done, ask a busy person to do it. Their suggestions, criticisms, and comments were insightful, detailed, and valuable. Each is the very model of a modern major editor. Michel's suggestions on what was then a long article were immensely useful. I am very much thankful—beholden may be a better word—to Nelson, who recommended, applying no pressure on me whatever, that I consider expanding the long article I had sent him for criticism and suggestions into a short book, and to Peter, whose various suggestions were all extremely profitable.

For permission to quote from the works of Bernard Shaw, I gratefully acknowledge the Society of Authors, on behalf of the Bernard Shaw Estate.

Praise for *Unions, Strikes, Shaw*

"An excellent book to put on the Bernard Shaw shelf that will serve a wider audience as well. Bernard F. Dukore's study is enlightening as it engages with recent scholarship to support questioning and provide answers that are fuller and better developed in specific contexts. It is well written and is high on my list of the most convincingly developed studies in this field. It fills an empty space in Shaw scholarship, and there's no need for, or likelihood that, another book would try to contest it."

—Richard F. Dietrich, *Professor Emeritus, University of South Florida, USA*

"Unions, Strikes, Shaw surveys general strikes, including the 1913 Dublin Lockout and 1926 British General Strike, and nationalization in Major Barbara and On the Rocks. Using Bernard Shaw's writings and speeches, and the words and actions of union organizers and members, government officials, and the public, this lively account illustrates how "unions, strikes and efforts by those in power to break them are as much a part of our lives as they were of Shaw's." Bernard F. Dukore has written extensively and perceptively on Shaw as social reformer, exploring crimes and punishments, censorship, and race. This thoroughly researched monograph is another valuable perspective on Shaw."

—Michel Pharand, *retired, freelance copyeditor and former general editor of SHAW: The Journal of Bernard Shaw Studies*

Note on Shaw

Bernard Shaw's idiosyncratic typographic style—such as omitting apostrophes from words like *you'd* and *doesn't*, whose meaning is clear without them—but distinguishing between *its* and *it's*, *cant* and *can't*, lest the former be considered misspellings, and using spaces within words or phrases rather than italics for emphasis—are retained in quotations.

Contents

CHAPTER 1

Introduction

Abstract The initial chapter treats the origins of this book and summarizes its contents, chapter by chapter.

Keywords Unions · Strikes · George Bernard Shaw · General Strike of 1926 · Gilded Age · Donald Trump · Margaret Thatcher · Ronald Reagan

Often, an introduction or preface to a book begins with an account of its origin. Robert A. Gaines, editor of *Bernard Shaw's Marriages and Misalliances*, entertainingly kicks off his preamble with: "The idea for this book was born when I reached for it on the library shelf, and it was not there." I wish I had as clever an opening as he does. Since I didn't, I settled for quoting his. Peter Gahan's *Bernard Shaw and Beatrice Webb on Poverty and Equality in the Modern World 1905–1914* starts with a reference to a "single golden thread [that] runs through the rich tapestry of Bernard Shaw's massive textual output," a strand to which insufficient attention has been paid and which he proceeds to rectify. Although part of my subject, which is expressed in this book's title, "runs through the rich tapestry" of Shaw's voluminous writings, to use Gahan's felicitous phrase, this book, as my tripartite title indicates, has no single thread.

B. F. Dukore, *Unions, Strikes, Shaw*,
Bernard Shaw and His Contemporaries,
https://doi.org/10.1007/978-3-030-99131-9_1

Shaw's voice is not present throughout. Some threads that permeate the book are far from golden. The strands running through its tapestry come not only from Shaw's writings and speeches, but also from the words and actions of union organizers, officials, and members, from the employers of the members and the lackies of the bosses, from national and municipal government officials, high and low, from journalists and experts on fields, and from the general public. Most of them were Shaw's contemporaries but some preceded his coevals. Other strands come, with what to some may be surprising appositeness, from our own contemporaries. In numerous respects, Shaw—who spent the first half of his life in the Victorian era—is also our contemporary.

As far as I can remember, the origins of this book were chiefly news stories and political commentaries during and after the most recent presidential election campaign in the United States, along with statements and actions by the former president and members of his administration while they were in office, and by his enablers in both houses of Congress—plus ample analysis by the commentariat of newspapers, magazines, and journals. The anti-union and anti-working-class statements and activities of the last decade almost continually reminded me of words and deeds in Shaw's time, by him and others. Words and actions by my present-day contemporaries struck me as a third act following a second act starring my earlier contemporaries, Margaret Thatcher and Ronald Reagan, and to a first act when the industrial revolution was under way—all part of the same real-life drama, or perhaps episodes in a series. To call the past, both recent and distant, pertinent to our time would be to understate. Thatcher's union-breaking actions, which she had planned well in advance of the strike by coal miners (on the basis of the secret Carrington report of 1978, six years before the strike commenced),[1] recalled the General Strike of 1926 in Britain, for which the government and mine owners, but not the unions and workers, had also planned in advance, and other general strikes in the United States and elsewhere long before she became prime minister—all of which figure prominently in this book. Like Great Britain, Europe, and the rest of the world, the United States has a history of government (state and city as well as national) support of individual owners and corporations in their disputes with unions and laborers. Reagan's and Donald Trump's efforts to revoke Franklin D. Roosevelt's New Deal (while claiming they supported ordinary people and were hostile to various elites, whatever the most recent of these presidents meant by the noun) took my mind back to the late nineteenth and early twentieth centuries, for we are in what Edward O'Donnell dubs Gilded Age 2.0—a term based on *The Gilded Age*, which Mark Twain and Dudley Warner coined for the title of their book, which was first published in 1873, during Victoria's reign, and which has become widely used for the twenty-first century. Like a gilded jewel it looks beautiful, but alongside and beneath the wealth it showcases are poverty, unemployment, vast inequality of income, and political corruption. As if to underscore parallels between Shaw's time and ours, the data analyzed by the UC Berkeley economist Emmanuel Saez shows that the income of the United States's top 10 percent averages more than nine times that of the bottom 90 percent, with that of the top 1 percent almost 40 percent higher. A 2021 article that cites his findings explicitly concludes, "U.S. inequality has returned to Gilded Age levels." In Twain's and Warner's day, as O'Donnell relates, steel created wealth, from railroads and architecture to medicine and consumer goods; now, the silicon chip and a digitized economy do so. Then as now, the ultra-wealthy had enormous estates of thousands of square feet, each property worth many million dollars. The opulent remain unapologetic, regardless of the wretched conditions of those living outside their estates.[2] Of this, more later. At present, it suffices to recognize the resemblance of the economic disparities of both gilded ages.

Do I exaggerate? Take such tweets as Trump's mini-rant of 29 April 2019, "I'll never get the support of Dues Crazy union leadership, those people who rip-off their membership with ridiculously high dues, medical and other expenses while being paid a fortune,"[3] which reveals more than his propensity for composing fiction. In pre-Trump times, the language was more elegant, or at least more polite, but the ideas were little different. Chapter 2 shows that Shaw addressed the subject of union dues in 1907. But "Dues Crazy" comes from the right-to-work playbook of 1944, when Reagan was a Hollywood actor, not a politician. Can this have anything to do with Shaw? It can. It does. As far back as 1909 the House of Lords delivered what has been called the Osborne Judgement, a landmark ruling which held that the law did not allow unions to collect money for political purposes, specifically to fund the new Labour Party's electoral efforts. Walter Osborne, a branch secretary of the union and a Liberal Party supporter, objected to the union's levy for political goals, since he was hostile to what he considered the "socialist" Labour

Party. The prominent Conservative politician Austen Chamberlain (half-brother of Neville Chamberlain, whose policy of appeasing Hitler remains notorious), who supported the Osborne Judgement, provided a purportedly apolitical reason based on personal rights: an individual unionist should not have his union use his dues to support a policy of a party not his own and of which he disapproves. When Shaw was asked in 1910 whether the Labour Party might get the decision reversed, he replied that the only recourse would be to pass a new Act making it legal for unions to maintain and pay election expenses of Labour candidates for Parliament—a recourse that is available, mutatis mutandis, to American state and federal legislatures. Impishly, Shaw pointed out that "a subscriber to the funds of the Unionist Party"—which broke from the Liberal Party to ally itself with the Conservative Party in opposition to Irish Home Rule—"who happens to be a Free Trader [which the Conservatives opposed] is in the same disagreeable position. It is an objection that applies more or less to all corporate action, and can only be escaped by living on a desert island." Chapter 9 will treat other aspects of this judgment from the Edwardian decade. In any case, Trump's three Executive Orders of 2 May 2018, titled in right-wing bureaucratese, were designed to break unions, which his Special Assistant for Domestic Policy, James Sherk, acknowledges in anodyne terminology as "a 'non-traditional labor legislative agenda'" before explicitly admitting their goals: to "sideline union leaders and eliminate all job protections for federal workers, including a requirement that federal contractors provide paid sick leave for employees" (see Chapters 4–6). Trump followed this agenda. As I have just suggested, the titles of these executive orders—"Cost-Reducing Approaches," "Taxpayer-Funded," and "Streamlining Removal [of personnel]"—are management-appropriate, not worker-appropriate.[4] The title of a 2020 article by two economists is "The Trump Administration's Attacks on Workplace Union Voting Rights Forewarned of the Broader Threats to Voting Rights in the Upcoming Election," and another article by them the same year (both one month before the 2020 election), states, "The suspension of union elections fits into a broader pattern of the Trump administration undermining workers' right to a union and democracy itself."[5]

Are we now in a post-Thatcher, post-Reagan, and post-Trump era? To quote what may be William Faulkner's most famous line, in *Requiem for a Nun*, "The past is never dead. It's not even past." The issues of unions, strikes, and efforts by those in power to break them are as much a part of our lives as they were of Shaw's, whose writings reflect them. As I have emphasized, they form tarnished threads, which like Gahan's golden thread have received insufficient attention. This book considers unionism, strikes and, in later chapters, nationalization in and before Shaw's time, and Shaw's attitudes toward these issues; and it also aims to offer insights into political disputes revolving around these topics in the more than seven decades after his death. The past is present still.

Chapter 2 contrasts attitudes toward unions in the time of Shaw's father, in Shaw's time twenty years later when he was a teenage clerk and in 1919, when he wrote about these times. He makes clear why unions are necessary for all wage earners, including clerks and writers. He himself had joined a union, the forerunner of the Society of Authors, three years after it had been founded, and he decried writers who worked against the interests of his union. Notwithstanding their necessity, he explains in the following chapter, he sees unions as antagonistic to business owners or employers, each hostile to the other—a view he portrays in the character of Snobby Price in *Major Barbara*. Although Shaw supported unions, as the former chapter attests, he also—perhaps paradoxically—opposed certain of their practices, including general strikes, which he considered reckless (he explicitly equated them with general suicides) and almost invariably doomed to failure for the striking workers, with adverse effects on the entire public as well.

Explaining the economics of the coal mining industry, the fourth chapter examines causes and actions—by both owners and their employed laborers—of several general strikes before and during Shaw's time, along with their outcomes, as well as the usual accompaniment of strikes, lock-outs, and violence, in the United States, Ireland, New Zealand, and European countries. This chapter, which is mainly background to Shaw, emphasizes the first two of the title's three words. His voice is first heard—loud, clear, and forcefully—late in the chapter, when we reach Dublin. Chapter 4 includes his insistence that near unanimity is required before a union calls for strike action. A majority of one, which is sufficient for an election, is insufficient to call a strike.

Chapter 5 provides a day by day analysis of one important industrial action, the General Strike of 1926, Great Britain's only such strike, which lasted a little more than a week. It began after the coal miners' union called for a vote, which was enormously positive. Miners then walked off the job and were joined by members of other unions in sympathetic action. It treats their aims and those of the conservative government, an uncompromising member of which was Winston Churchill, in addition to the government's flagrant hostility toward the strikers and its use of the Royal Army and Navy to crush them, as well as lockouts and other tactics by the mine owners. This chapter records the strike's humiliating failure, its disastrous results, and its aftermath. Shaw's voice is absent from this chapter. To maintain the focus on this strike, I reserve his opinions about it for the next chapter.

Thus, the concentration of Chapter 6 is on Shaw's views of the 1926 General Strike, almost none of which he publicly expressed while it was happening. He made them known chiefly in a major work, *The Intelligent Woman's Guide to Socialism and Capitalism*, a best-seller that he wrote during the strike and that he published two years after it collapsed. Promoting nationalization of industries (which the country did not realize it had in certain services) as desirable, although less desirable than socialism, he dismisses strikes, which unions still call labor's only weapon, as useless for both the workers and the national interest. In a general strike, he warns, because capitalists can hold out longer than workers can, unions, whose reserve funds are more limited, habitually lose.

In Chapter 7 Shaw contrasts socialism and nationalization, and he explains the superiority of Fabianism in its ability to achieve the former. This chapter includes his dramatization of social improvement before the arrival of socialism in his dialectical play *Major Barbara*.

Chapter 8 also focuses on nationalization, this time in the political arena, and it examines Shaw's only play whose prominent themes are the subjects of this book: *On the Rocks*, written and first performed during the Great Depression, when literally millions of Britons were out of work. Recognizing that nationalization and municipalization would solve the nation's economic dilemmas, the play's prime minister sets forth a program that includes nationalizing ground rent, municipalizing urban land, and replacing taxes and tariffs with foreign trade in state-protected industries whose products the state would sell at regulated prices, with profits, if any, accruing to the country. The government would pay for its actions by such measures as doubling the surtax on income derived from investments and abolishing inheritance taxes; and it would, in accordance with British laws and traditions, give compensation to owners of confiscated property.

The final chapter summarizes Shaw's solutions and explores whether and under what circumstances, political and administrative, they may be valid. It continues through Prime Minister Clement Attlee's postwar Labour government, which nationalized coal mining and other vital industries. It examines the soundness of objections to nationalization and to comparably large or larger private industries. Following this, it deals with strikes and privatization in the U.K. and the United States as well as with union-breaking actions by Margaret Thatcher, Ronald Reagan and Donald Trump, adumbrated in this chapter, relating them to union-management conflicts when Shaw was alive and active, and to statements and actions treated in previous chapters. In addition, it offers an example, in *Major Barbara*, of the gap between the top income percentile and those far below it.

Notes

1. Peter Hennessy, "Mrs. Thatcher Warned in Secret Report of Defeat in Confrontation with Unions," *The Times*, 18 April 1978, reprinted in "Strikes," *Thatcher Foundation*, https://www.margaretthatcher.org/document/111396.
2. Edward T. O'Donnell, "Are We Living in the Gilded Age 2.0?" *History*, 31 January 2019, https://www.history.com/news/second-gilded-age-income-inequality; "Facts: Income Inequality in the United States," *Inequality*, https://inequality.org/facts/income-inequality/.
3. "Donald Trump's Public Statements on Issue: Labor Unions," *Vote Smart*, https://justfacts.votesmart.org/candidate/public-statements/15723/donald-trump/43/labor-unions.
4. "The Secret White House Memo: Inside Trump's Plan to Destroy Unions," *Labor Tribune*, 19 November 2019, https://labortribune.com/the-secret-white-house-memo-inside-trumps-plan-to-destroy-unions/; "Executive Orders 13836, 13837, and 13839: A Presidential Document by the Executive Office of the President on 10/21/2019," *Federal Register: The Daily Journal of the United States Government*, https://www.federalregister.gov/documents/2019/10/21/2019-23021/executive-orders-13836-13837-and-13839.
5. James G. Moher, "The Osborne Judgement of 1909: Trade Union Funding of Political Parties in Historical Perspective," *History & Policy*, 2 December 2009, https://www.historyandpolicy.org/policy-papers/papers/the-osborne-judgement-of-1909-trade-union-funding-of-political-parties-in-h; George Bernard Shaw, "Mr. Bernard Shaw, Special Interview," *The Freeman's Journal*, 3 October 1910: 7; Celine McNicholas and Margaret

Poydock, "The Trump Administration's Attacks on Workplace Union Voting Rights Forewarned of the Broader Threats to Voting Rights in the Upcoming Election," *Economic Policy Institute*, 21 October 2020, https://www.epi.org/publication/the-trump-administrations-attacks-on-workplace-union-voting-rights-forewarned-of-the-broader-threats-to-voting-rights-in-the-upcoming-election/; Celine McNicholas and Margaret Poydock, "The Trump Administration's Union Election Suspension at Pandemic's Onset Impacted Nearly 17,000 Workers," *Economic Policy Institute*, 21 October 2020, https://www.epi.org/press/the-trump-administrations-union-election-suspension-at-pandemics-onset-impacted-nearly-17000-workers/.

CHAPTER 2

Bernard Shaw, Union Member

Abstract Shaw commanded high fees for his writings but accepted little or no payment for his obligation to his profession, writing, and to the union that represented its members. A former clerk when he was a teenager in Dublin, he explained attitudes toward unions then, in his father's time and the present day; and he urged readers who were clerks to join their professional union. He clarified why unions were necessary to all wage earners. He joined the Society of Authors three years after it was founded, worked on its committees, defended the necessity of unions, and decried writers who opposed and worked against the interests of union members.

Keywords Unions · George Bernard Shaw

In a letter to the actor Robert Loraine, on 6 January 1909, Shaw wrote, "I have two prices: one for American magazines and the other for English ones, the proportion being as high as 8 to 1 or even much more. For instance I am writing an article on Poe for [Henry William] Massingham (*The Nation*), and shall take what he can afford—possibly nothing, possibly 12 guineas, at the utmost, £25. But for an American magazine I should expect up to £200."[1] Shaw sounds like a high-priced

B. F. Dukore, *Unions, Strikes, Shaw*,
Bernard Shaw and His Contemporaries,
https://doi.org/10.1007/978-3-030-99131-9_2

lawyer who also does *pro bono* work. In 1919 he wrote a preface to *Trade Unionism for Clerks*. The following year he slightly revised it for William Randolph Hearst, who provided him with a far larger audience in the United States, signed it "G. Bernard Shaw (ex-clerk)" and retitled it for American readers, "The Clerk and Emperor of China: Why I Have Joined a Trade Union."[2] Whereas he likely wrote "A Foreword to the Clerks" for no payment or for a token fee, Hearst paid top dollar. Since the original is reprinted in a more accessible book, I cite it. Because the article is autobiographical—or perhaps the movie credit "inspired by true events" is more accurate—and amusing, I treat it at length. I should note here that whereas, in earlier times, trade unions had developed in order to represent only skilled workers, since their organizers and members considered unskilled workers inferior to them, other unions then arose for unskilled and relatively unskilled workers, who were in the majority, and for female workers, and these other unions eventually merged with trade unions, which came to include both the skilled and the unskilled, both men and women.[3] Here, except in quotations, I use "unions" and "trade unions" interchangeably.

Shaw relates that in Dublin, from 1871 to 1876, he was an office clerk. Then, two types of workers were almost impossible to organize, women and clerks, because neither hoped to stay at their jobs. "The woman intended to get married and have a house of her own and be her own mistress, no matter how poor she was. The clerk either hated business and meant to get out of it and become a great man" or if he liked business he meant to set up one of his own unless the boss made him a partner. To Shaw's contemporaries, his position was good. His firm valued his work and raised his salary. His job could have launched him to a respectable career. If there had been a trade union of clerks he would not have joined it. Not only was it thought ungentlemanly, "it would have been stupid, because I should not have intended to remain a clerk, but to employ clerks." His view would have been the employer's, as became a man who was convinced he would become either an employer or a failure. Forty years later, having "pulled off the Great Man Stunt" and been "held up to an admiring Europe as 'the Molière of the Twentieth Century'" (the title of a 1913 book by Augustin Hamon, his French translator), he needed a Commissioner of Oaths to witness a legal document. By chance, he claims, he was standing outside his old Dublin office. The commissioner was not in, but his clerk was—a man who coincidentally (enter Shaw the raconteur?) had been employed there when he was. When Shaw told him this, the clerk said, "'*I don't remember you*'" (italics are in the original). In the intervening years, "whilst I was making six or seven reputations, touching nothing that I did not adorn, being abused by all the papers as only the famous are abused, and surveying mankind, if not from China to Peru, at least from [Istanbul] to Jamaica," the clerk worked from 10 a.m. to 5 p.m., which Shaw would have done, but for the "accident of my turning out to be the one man in every million or so who happens to have the knack of telling lies so attractively that people go to the theater to see actors pretending that they all are true." He could not believe that when they were youths in the 1870s the clerk hoped to be a clerk all his life any more than Shaw did. "I fled from his majestic presence recalling many memories."

Shaw reflected on clerkship forty years earlier, when his father had employed clerks. If his own chances of "becoming an employer were ten to one in 1870, you may take the chances against the clerk of today as a thousand to one." In Shaw's father's time joint stock companies ran three businesses: banking, insurance, and railways. In Shaw's day as a clerk limited liability companies ran a third of Britain's businesses. Today trusts have superseded such companies, carrying on banking amalgamations along with tobacco shops. Managers and clerks are now employees. If one of them wanted to start on his own he would need a hundred thousand pounds for each pound his father had, and even then he would have a slim chance if he tried to compete with trusts instead of making it worth their while to acquire his firm. Whereas the old-time clerk could neither type nor do shorthand, he could read, write and do arithmetic; mechanics and laborers did not know the alphabet or how to write their names. The clerk had a monopoly with no competition outside his class. Anyone who could read and write presentably was regarded as a gentleman. Now, children of mechanics are better educated for business purposes than King Edward VII was. Almost every boy is more or less qualified for clerkship when he finishes school, and competition is less ruinous than before, since skilled trades absorb thousands of boys whom "Victorian snobbery would have condemned to the desk." Even so, competition is so heavy that clerks, like their employers, try to better themselves. Fifty years ago employers stopped competing and started combining. A hundred years ago mechanics and laborers did this. But many clerks still cling to the policy of "playing for promotion to the employing class, not realizing that nowadays an average clerk's chance of getting there is about as great as his chance of becoming Emperor of China." Yet clerking is better than before.

Today's big company or combine pays managing clerks more than they could have made in business for themselves years ago and ordinary clerks more than a small employer could have afforded. "It has to consider the health and efficiency of its clerks: a thing that never entered the head of an old-time employer." Today few managing clerks are not better off than Shaw's father was as a partner. Yet there are downsides. If Shaw's father's clerk had a complaint he might tell it to Shaw's good-natured, reasonable parent, who "could ease the harness when it galled." A modern clerk cannot complain to a trust, which is "a huge impersonal aggregation of capital, where his immediate superior is an employee like himself," and to do anything for one clerk means doing it for a hundred or a thousand others. If Shaw's father raised the clerk's salary to a pound a month, the cost was twelve pounds a year. To today's establishments a salary increase of a pound a month for one clerk would mean a total of twelve thousand a year for all clerks, which makes the individual clerk helpless. This does not mean the father's clerk was safer. Each office had so few clerks that the employer could "'sack the lot'" and get new clerks the next day, or do the job himself for a week. "But a Trust cannot sack the lot. It cannot carry on for half a day without them." Nor can it sack only one if the clerks are united, as railway workers and coal miners are.

Shaw gives "the moral of my tale. First make up your mind that nowadays once an employee always an employee." Even a small-scale employer will likely be taken over by a trust and made an employee. "Second, realize that as an individual you are now utterly helpless." If you want a raise, shorter hours or "any amelioration whatsoever in the conditions of your employment, you must ask it not only for yourself but for all the other clerks as well; and you have no authority to ask in their name... even if you could get at any supreme individual from whom you could ask it." Unless you make a demand officially through a union of clerks you cannot make it. Therefore, "join the National Union of Clerks [which is now called the Association of Professional, Executive, Clerical and Computer Staff] before you have time to cool down about it." If he were a clerk he would "join it without a moment's hesitation, just as I have joined my own Trade Union, the Society of Authors, Playwrights, and Composers."

Shaw did so in August 1897, three years after it was founded. It still exists as the Society of Authors (in 1905 the composers broke off to form their own union). He plunged into union activities. In October, half a year before *Plays: Pleasant and Unpleasant* was first published in 1898, he suggested to Henry Arthur Jones, an established, popular commercial dramatist, which Shaw was not, and who was chairman of the society's dramatic subcommittee, that the society set a minimum price for plays to end the freelancing that goes on through the ignorance of authors. He recognized the difficulty of finding time for union work, but "it ought to be done." Jones and he can "pit our individual wit and strength" against successful managers, "but the small fry are bound to crumple up without an organization behind them."[4] In 1903 he wrote a letter to the *Saturday Review*, for which he had been the theater reviewer less than ten years earlier. In it, he called attention to editors who were "not men of letters, but simply exploiters of men of letters," "papers which care more for the advertisements of the members of the Publishers' Association than for the status of the professional writer," and "journalists so abject that they will write articles and paragraphs to help such editors and such papers to damage the Authors' Society." Writers with no sense "of esprit de corps, of loyalty to poorer comrades... care nothing for the less fortunate people out of whom books are sweated on terms that would drive a matchbox maker to strike." For only a guinea a year the Society offers its members the services of solicitors who know literary business, which ordinary solicitors do not, and the secretary who knows more about it than solicitors do. The better type of men of letters join a professional association not for what they can get from it but "because they know that the rights of the whole community of authors must be sustained by a permanent organisation which, by being ready to meet all attacks, prevents attacks from being made." While non-dues-payers "sponge on its activity or enjoy its protection," honorable writers "do not take advantage of this: they pay, and take their turns on the committees when they are wanted."[5]

Three years later, at the annual dinner of the Society of Authors, he called literature "a sweated trade," which is one reason the society exists. In industry at its worst, "the employer, instead of having the work done in his own factory, gives it out to workers who do it in their own homes." This is universal "in our literary industry." Sweating, which is common among writers, is competition by subsidized labor, notably by married women. If women at the dinner are among them, "I cannot too earnestly implore them never to accept a cheque for a piece of literary work without asking themselves whether, if they were single women, with nothing but their pens between them and starvation, or worse still, widows with children depending on them, the sum would be sufficient to support them in reasonable decency during the time occupied by the work." Without a union, writers are helpless. At the start of their career "we are so poor and so busy that we have neither the time nor the means to defend ourselves against the commercial organisations which exploit us." When they achieve fame, they leap from being too poor to fight to having time too valuable to waste on lawsuits. But, union member Shaw declares, "We all, eminent and obscure alike, need the Authors' Society. We all owe it a share of our time, our means, our influence." It is of greater service to those who never use it than those with cases contested by the society's secretary, whose expertise prevents cases from arising.[6]

Before proceeding to the chapters that follow, we should recognize that members of both unions dealt with in this chapter are white-collar workers, that these unions have much fewer members than trade unions or unions of unskilled workers have, and that their impact on the nation's day-to-day businesses and the lives of its people is less than unions of blue-collar workers. Shaw's distinction between the latter's greater numbers and more far-reaching consequences of their actions may partly account for seemingly paradoxical attitudes toward unions.

Notes

1. *My Dear Loraine: Bernard Shaw's Letters to an Actor*, ed. L.W. Conolly (Niagara-on-the-Lake, ON: Shaw Festival, 2020), p. 13.
2. Bernard Shaw, "A Foreword to the Clerks," *Trade Unionism for Clerks*, reprinted Bernard Shaw, *Complete Prefaces*, ed. Dan H. Laurence and Daniel J. Leary (London: Allen Lane, 1995), Vol. 2, pp. 308–13; G. Bernard Shaw, "The Clerk and Emperor of China: Why I Have Joined a Trade Union," *Hearst's Magazine*, 37 (January 1920): 14, 78.
3. William English Walling, "The New Unionism—The Problem of the Unskilled Worker," *Annals of the American Academy of Political and Social Science*, 24 (September 1904): 12–13, 21–22.
4. Bernard Shaw, *Collected Letters*, ed. Dan H. Laurence (London: Max Reinhardt, 1965–88), Vol. 1, pp. 812–13.
5. G. Bernard Shaw, "The Society of Scribes," *Saturday Review*, 95 (14 March 1903): 326.
6. Bernard Shaw, "The Annual Dinner," *The Author*, 5 (June 1906): 268–70.

CHAPTER 3

Unions and *Major Barbara*

Abstract Despite Shaw's favorable view of unionism, he also held an adverse attitude toward unions, which lasted for the remainder of his ninety-four-year-old life. He was militant, advising workers to stick to their unions when they battled business owners or employers, but he was hostile to unions as well, because capitalism has corrupted both antagonists, compelling each to act in its own behalf, not in the public's. He dramatized this view in *Major Barbara*.

Keywords Unions · George Bernard Shaw · *Major Barbara*

Despite Shaw's advocacy of unions, which is the subject of the last chapter, he used unions as whipping boys—giving him the appearance, at the very least, of an unconventional and odd advocate of unions. Since married women are dependent on their husbands, he has Don Juan, in *Man and Superman* (1902), ask, "What is virtue but the Trade Unionism of the married?" and in the preface (1908) to *Getting Married*, he argues that wedlock "reduces the difference between marriage and prostitution to the difference between Trade Unionism and unorganized prostitution."[1] In 1900 he called it "the duty of every trade to organize in order to make war upon and rob the rest of society"—an obligation almost

B. F. Dukore, *Unions, Strikes, Shaw*,
Bernard Shaw and His Contemporaries,
https://doi.org/10.1007/978-3-030-99131-9_3

guaranteed to create interest in, if not shock, the readers of the newspaper in which it appeared, the popular *Daily Mail*, which at the time had a circulation of half a million, a number that more than doubled two years later. This was not a view customary in a halfpenny paper (other newspapers at the time were usually one penny). Shaw was serious. To him, at least at that time, intimidation by unions was legitimate. Bringing the subject to his own profession, he argued, with comic hyperbole, that if he "offered to write an article for a guinea and another man came along and offered to do it for half, I should be justified in assassinating the other man." And with amusing earnestness he advised workers, "Waste as much as you can, do your work as badly as you can, and idle as much as you can, without absolutely getting the sack." He told them to stick to their union "as long as it tries to control the output, and ruin the master." If it becomes respectable or moderate, a worker "'may be sure that it is doing him no good, and he should drop it at once and join some other organization where he can be certain the officials... have no scruples about benefiting him at the expense of other people.'"[2] As he reiterated to his biographer, Archibald Henderson, shortly thereafter, the goal of trade unions is "to get as much out of the employer and give him as little in return as possible, precisely as the employer's method is to get as much out of his employees and give them as little in return as he can without killing the goose that lays the golden eggs." Capitalism corrupts the worker as well as the employer. Each acts for himself.[3]

If these statements have a familiar ring it is because Shaw used them in *Major Barbara* (1905). "I stand by my class and do as little as I can so's to leave arf the job for me fellow workers," says Snobby Price in the play. "I'm fly enough to know wots inside the law and wots outside it; and inside it I do as the capitalists do: pinch wot I can lay me ends on."[4] We are accustomed to witty or urbane characters enunciating Shaw's views but not to rascals doing so. Snobby's real name (Bronterre O'Brien, a Chartist leader) is a clue to his views, but he is so clearly a liar (he publicly claims that he beat his mother, whereas he privately confesses that she beat him—which the 1941 movie version dramatizes) and a thief (in play and film he steals the pound Undershaft put on the Salvation Army drum), we are unlikely to consider him a raisonneur. In this case he is. As Shaw told Gabriel Pascal, director of the movie version, the actor should "contrast... the smart cockney talking honestly to Rummy, and the snivelling canting mock-pious hypocrite when the others are present."[5] Snobby is not the type of proletarian who regards those who consider what Shaw calls the proprietariat—a word he coined—as worthy of respect and privileges, or as especially honorable, and he would rob them with the approval of his conscience if their social positions were reversed. A malcontent, he neither obeys his rulers nor submits to them, because his conscience is the same as theirs.[6] The year before Shaw wrote *Major Barbara*, he phrased Snobby's view in a manner to which we are more accustomed. The antagonism between the proletariat and the proprietariat, he said, is between the seller and the buyer of labor; and the success of unionism represents not socialism but the interests of the seller of labor as opposed to those of the buyer of labor.[7]

In 1926, the year he received the Nobel Prize for 1925, Shaw tried to standardize Snobby's view in the *Encyclopædia Britannica*, where his essay "Socialism" defines trade unionism as "a phase of capitalism, inasmuch as it applies to labour as a commodity that principle of selling in the dearest market, and giving as little as possible for the price," which is usually applied only to capitalism. "Its method is that of a civil war between labour and capital in which the decisive battles are lock-outs and strikes, with intervals of minor adjustment by industrial diplomacy."[8] In 1941 he explained this in less off-putting terms: although trade unionism calls itself socialist and adopts "parliamentary methods as well as direct action by strikes," it is not socialist: it aims "to exploit the capitalist system so as to secure the lion's share of its product for the proletarian Trade Unionists instead of for the landlords and capitalists."[9] He treats these issues more fully in *The Intelligent Woman's Guide to Socialism and Capitalism*, which I will analyze in Chapter 6.

At present, it is important to recognize Shaw's belief that unions would insufficiently guarantee gains for workers. Hovering in the background, Peter Gahan pointed out to me, was the Fabian campaign as early as 1888 to 1893 for an eight-hour working day, which had the Eight Hours bill for miners as its focus (in nineteenth-century Britain the working day was usually ten hours, and often more, for six days a week). The Fabians supported the Liberal Party in the general election of 1892 on the basis that its program included such progressive measures as an eight-hour working day. As Edward Pease said in 1916, "English Socialism had come into being and Trade Unionism had been transformed by the rise of the Dockers, and the other 'new' unions of unskilled labour." Since "a Labour Party was in the future," the *Fabian Election Manifesto* (1892), written by Shaw, "bluntly [told] the working classes that until they form a party of their own they will have to choose between the parties belonging to the other classes." In March 1893 Henry Campbell-Bannerman, who had pledged that the government would become "'the best employers of labour in the country,'" revealed that, in Pease's words, "enunciating a principle is one thing, and carrying it into effect in scores of departments is another." When no legislation on this matter was forthcoming, Shaw wrote "To Your Tents, Oh Israel!" with suggestions from Sidney Webb (the title is from 1 Kings 12: when King David did not listen to the Israelites, they told him to go his tent—go home, that is, or go away—and left him to go to their own tents, that is, to look after themselves). Shaw wrote: "The first question the trade unionist asks of a government is, 'Are you a "rat" house or are you a fair house?' And by this he means, 'Do you pay starvation wages and keep your men working sweaters' hours; or do you pay trade union rates, prohibit overtime, and observe the eight-hour day?'" With a few strokes of a pen, the government could have modified contracts that had mail cart drivers work fourteen hours a day, made "the postmen's nominal eight hours a day a reality, and... extend[ed] its operation to the artisans in the Post office and Telegraph stores and workshops." The War Office could have done the same, as other public departments could have. Campbell-Bannerman, he charged, "uses fair words about the eight-hour day" but "he has done nothing...." Pease points out that Shaw "showed in considerable detail how a Labour Party ought to be formed, and how, in fact, it was formed seven years later." The article's publication in the *Fortnightly Review* in November 1893 broke the link with the Liberals that the Fabians had nurtured since 1885, and it led to the revision and expansion of the essay into *Fabian Tract 49*, *A Plan of Campaign for Labor* (1894), which became the blueprint for a Trades Unions financed Labour Party to represent working people's interests in parliament.[10]

Notes

1. Bernard Shaw, *Collected Plays with Their Prefaces*, ed. Dan H. Laurence (London: Max Reinhardt, 1971), 2: 670, 3: 501.
2. "Tyranny Indeed: Mr. Bernard Shaw's Advice to Trade Union Workmen," *Daily Mail*, 24 November 1900, p. 3.
3. Archibald Henderson, *Table-Talk of G.B.S.* (New York: Harper & Brothers, 1925), pp. 153–54.
4. Bernard Shaw, *Major Barbara*, *Collected Plays with Their Prefaces*, ed. Dan H. Laurence (London: Max Reinhardt, 1971), Vol. 3, p. 96.

5. *Bernard Shaw and Gabriel Pascal*, ed. Bernard F. Dukore (Toronto: University of Toronto Press, 1996), p. 103.
6. Bernard Shaw, *The Intelligent Woman's Guide to Socialism and Capitalism* (London: Constable, 1928), p. 223. In 1937 Shaw expanded and retitled the book. I cite the expanded edition, *The Intelligent Woman's Guide to Socialism, Capitalism, Sovietism and Fascism* (London: Constable, 1949), also p. 223. Valerie Adams credits Shaw for having coined the word—Valerie Adams, *An Introduction to Modern English Word-Formation* (London: Routledge, 2016 [first published 1973]), p. 163—and although she cites Webster's *Third International Dictionary* (1961) as precedent in crediting him (Adams, p. 168), my 1968 edition of the book does not; but it credits him for "proprietarian." Yet the *Compact Edition of the Oxford English Dictionary: A Supplement to the Oxford English Dictionary* (1987), credits him, citing *The Intelligent Woman's Guide to Socialism.*
7. George Bernard Shaw, "The Class War," *The Clarion* (30 September 1904), p. 5.
8. George Bernard Shaw, "George Bernard Shaw on Socialism," *Encyclopædia Britannica*, 6 November 2014, https://www.britannica.com/topic/George-Bernard-Shaw-on-socialism-1985101.
9. "A Message from Bernard Shaw," *Labour Monthly*, 23 (July 1941): 305–6.
10. Peter Gahan email to me, 24 June 2021; he reveals that "To Your Tents, Oh Israel!" will be, and now has been, reprinted in the forthcoming issue of *SHAW: The Journal Bernard Shaw Studies*, 41.2 (2021), ed. Nelson O'Cellaigh Ritschell and him; Edward R. Pease, *History of the Fabian Society: The Origins of English Socialism* (St. Petersburg, FL: Red and Black Publishers, n.d.), pp. 84–88; Bernard Shaw, *A Plan of Campaign for Labour, Which Contains "To Your Tents, Oh Israel!," Fabian Tract 49* (London: The Fabian Society, 1894), pp. 4–6, http://webbs.library.lse.ac.uk/972/.

CHAPTER 4

Background: General Strikes and the Dublin Lockout of 1913

Abstract To Shaw, general strikes amounted to general suicides. This chapter examines their causes, actions, and outcomes in the United States—not only by coal miners and railroad workers, from the Great Railroad Strike of Philadelphia to mining strikes in Idaho, centered in Coeur d'Alene, and the Seattle General Strike. It includes activities, legal and not, violent and not, by owners, workers, unions and employer organizations, governors and presidents or prime ministers, plus outcomes—as well general strikes in Europe, Great Britain, and Dublin, where general strikes precipitated lockouts by employers. This chapter includes Shaw's view of the general strike as a "thoughtless absurdity" and the need for militancy in the event of a lockout, as well as the requirement of near unanimity in calling one out. It also treats economic problems of coal mining during and after World War I.

Keywords Unions, general strikes in Britain, the United States and New Zealand · The Dublin Lockout of 1913 · The French railway strikes of 1920 · The Seattle General Strike of 1919 · The Coal Miners' Strike of 1892 · The Coeur d'Alene Miners' Strikes · Lyons Tea Shops strike · George Bernard Shaw

B. F. Dukore, *Unions, Strikes, Shaw*,
Bernard Shaw and His Contemporaries,
https://doi.org/10.1007/978-3-030-99131-9_4

Shaw regarded strikes that affect millions as catastrophes. This is especially true of work stoppages like the British General Strike of 1926, the nation's first and only one. He made his disapprobation of general strikes clear five years before it: "A general strike is a general suicide."[1] As I have indicated in Chapter 1, this chapter is primarily devoted to selected worldwide strikes (plus lockouts) and unions, which from a Shavian view are, as the title of this chapter makes clear, background to Shaw, whose voice first arrives late in the section, when we come to a strike and lockout at his *ville natale*, where it is strong and militant. We hear it again in relation to the country whose language I just used to characterize Dublin. Details of these unquestionably important labor disputes and strikes of which Shaw appears to have said nothing or little are important as background to the labor issues and strikes of which he spoke. He learned from the labor clashes of both, and he vigorously argued, for example, that decisions to call strikes, such as railroad strikes in France, which took place not long afterward, must meet a significant criterion that is different from elections. For the possibility of a strike's success, a majority of one or ten or even a hundred, which can make an election succeed, offers a prospect of failure to strikers. The mere potential of success, he insisted, demands the virtually unanimous approval of union members who are called out to strike.

In the United States the first general strike took place before Shaw was born. It occurred in Philadelphia and was led by the General Trades' Union (GTU). It started in May 1835, impromptu, when coal heavers of the docks struck for a ten-hour workday. Shoemakers, carpenters, and other tradesmen joined, crying, "We are all day laborers!" For a week the GTU leaders used the press, posters, and parades to rally workers. More than forty trades and almost twenty thousand workers united. By the end of June most laborers won the concessions they demanded; and the GTU embraced unskilled workers, who also received a ten-hour workday. For seven months after the general strike, every strike succeeded, but afterwards many workers left the union and met a backlash from employers who formed associations to defeat strikers. With the financial panic of 1837, banks and businesses collapsed, workers lost their jobs and the GTU died.[2]

Almost all general strikes in Europe and the United States failed. American presidents refused to intervene or intervened on the side of the owners in railroad strikes (1877 and 1894) and mining strikes (1892 and 1899) by sending in the National Guard. In 1865, when the United

States Civil War ended, there were 35,000 miles of railroad tracks; on the eve of World War I, 254,000 miles. Not only was the Great Railroad Strike of 1877 the nation's first major rail strike, it was also the country's first general strike. This rail strike, the strikes that followed, and the violence they generated so paralyzed the nation's businesses that governors of ten states mobilized 60,000 members of their militias to reopen railroad traffic. In 1877 railroads in the north were still trying to cope with fallout from the Financial Panic of 1873. Employers made use of the usual methods, cutting wages and salaries, with the usual consequences, strikes, and violence. In May the Pennsylvania Railroad Company, the largest in the country, cut wages by 10 percent; in June by another 10 percent. Other railroad companies did the same; some also cut the work week to two or three days, which prompted firemen to walk off the job. Baltimore and West Virginia workers blockaded freight trains, allowing only passenger traffic to move (the former were more profitable to the companies, the latter better known to, therefore more popular with the public). When the Pennsylvania Railroad planned to double the length of trains from Pittsburgh without increasing the number of men in the crews, workers seized control of the railway switches, which allowed trains to change tracks, thereby preventing the trains from moving. Ferocious strikes erupted throughout the country, including in major hubs, such as Chicago, St. Louis, and San Francisco. Governors called out state militias. When Pittsburgh's militia sympathized with the city's railway workers, the governor sent troops from Philadelphia, which is over three hundred miles away, who fired into the crowd, killing more than twenty, including women and children. Invoking the American Revolution and the Bible, a newspaper headline announced, "Shot in Cold Blood by the Roughs of Philadelphia. The Lexington of the Labor Conflict at Hand. The Slaughter of Innocents." The crowd forced the Philadelphian soldiers to retreat to a roundhouse, and it set fire to buildings, engines, and equipment. A twenty-year-old member of the Maryland National Guard, which would arrive soon, described one rampage: "We met a mob, which blocked the streets. They came armed with stones and as soon as we came within reach they began to throw [them] at us." The armed and bayoneted militia killed ten people, including a newsboy and a sixteen-year-old student, thereby initiating a riot. Demonstrators burned a passenger car, caused a locomotive to crash into freight cars, and cut fire hoses. In this battle 14,000 men rioted. What happened was clear to the Baltimoreans, one of whom, a businessman, anonymously wrote that the strike was "not a revolution of fanatics willing to fight for an idea. It is a revolt of working men against low prices of labor, which have not been accomplished with corresponding low prices of food, clothing and house rent." Maryland's governor, who did not see it that way, telegraphed President Rutherford B. Hayes, asking him to send troops to defend the city. In fact, the Great Railroad Strike was the first time a president used federal troops to break strikes—a power derived from constitutional and statutory provisions authorizing the use of armed forces to help suppress domestic violence and insurrection, to protect federal property, and carry out federal laws or court orders. Its use is discretionary. The president is the only authority to decide whether to send in troops, which means whether to help defeat the strikers or assist them. While presidents did both, the latter was a drop in the bucket.[3]

Although unions had a history in coal mining in the United States, no successful national union was established until 1890. During the economic depression of the 1870s various unions were founded, had unsuccessful strikes, and then collapsed. In the mid-1880s, local organizations joined the Knights of Labor, whose local chapters were often secret. The Knights of Labor was the most important union of that decade, but when it led a four-state strike against railroad baron Jay Gould in 1886, for better wages and treatment, he used police against the strikers and thus wrecked the union. In those decades local unions tried repeatedly to found a national union. In late 1885 miners succeeded, ironically, in forming two competing national unions. In December 1888 the two unions merged, quarreled, and finally united on 22 January 1890 as the United Mine Workers of America (UMW). The unions were not as powerful as the miners wanted them to be and they did not have enough financial resources for a strike fund. From 1881 to 1894, coal miners received an average of $1.39 per worker in union-called strikes. A nonunion striker got only 65 cents. After 1886 the mean financial assistance in union-called strikes in bituminous coal mining was lower than before ($1.20). Moreover, the local union chapters did not directly furnish most of the financial aid. Money for striking workers came principally from unions in other, sometimes faraway states, contributions from private individuals and donations from individual miners elsewhere, and from different labor organizations. The coal miners' union had to rely on ad hoc committees to collect money. This did not change until much later. Only one strike had significant union contributions: the Connellsville Coke Field, Ohio, strike in early 1891, where miners received $300,000;

but after this, the union had no money to join the eight-hour movement announced for 1 May.[4]

The miners' strikes of 1892 and 1899 are related to each other. Before 1891 all mines in the Coeur d'Alene region of northern Idaho had worked to capacity, all had earned good dividends, men who used dynamite to blast holes in the rocks to create mine shafts got three dollars and fifty cents a day, and "muckers" (men who shoveled broken rock into underground tramming cars) fifty cents less. There were no unions. Members of the Mine Owners' Association, formed in 1891, regarded unionization as something that outside agitators (from such cities as Butte, Montana) tried to impose. This organization precipitated a series of events that the miners considered throwing down the gauntlet, especially since one of its first moves was to employ the Pinkerton and Thiel detective agencies to place spies in the union. Literally, 1892 began with war between coal owners and miners. On 1 January the owners closed the mines and told the miners that higher freight rates by the railroads made mining unprofitable. On 1 April, after the owners negotiated lower freight rates, they reopened the mines but claimed that low silver and lead prices prevented them from paying the earlier uniform wages. They proposed rates between $3.50 and $3.00, which they had paid from 1887 to 1891. After a long winter with no pay the union miners were disinclined to have their wage gains obliterated, rejected the owners' offer, also rejected a so-called compromise differential rate, and went on strike. Two large mines settled, opened with union workers, and operated at full scale, but other mine owners, who wanted no union, ostracized their operators. The miners declared a strike against reduced wages and increased work hours. The owners were just as adamant. Within a month they recruited strikebreakers and brought them to the district. Groups of armed, striking miners frequently met incoming trains that carried their intended replacements and often persuaded them not to take jobs during the strike. Local pro-miner railroad men arranged for special trains with strikebreakers which took them two hundred miles away from their destination. Union miners also boarded incoming passenger trains in Coeur d'Alene to ensure that no scabs got off. The mine managers countered by getting an injunction that ordered miners not to interfere with their obtaining nonunion employees for the mines. Tensions increased. The miners controlled the government of the communities—one-street towns at the foot of canyons, with no detours—through which newly arriving strikebreakers arrived.

The mine owners responded by hiring armed guards to accompany nonunion workers. The situation was explosive.[5]

On 10 July a union miner and a strikebreaker had a fist fight, which sparked a rumor that scabs had killed two union members. This triggered greater violence on the 11th. At the Frisco mine gunfire was exchanged between miners and guards, each group claiming the other had fired first. Eventually the union men poured a box of black powder through a chute into a four-story mill, the explosion leveling it, killing one company man and injuring others. The union miners fired into the structure where the guards were sheltering. A second company man was killed and sixty guards surrendered. Minutes after the explosion, the armed miners searched for Charlie Siringo, a Pinkerton detective they particularly despised. He slipped out of town. Taking to the hills to find him, the miners shot at all the strikebreakers they saw, killing at least one. Company forces evacuated another mine and hundreds of union men converged on still another, which was also evacuated. The victorious union miners ordered nonunion men to leave the area and threatened to blow up the mine's concentrator if they did not. On 12 July the owners ordered their nonunion men to leave town. About 130 nonunion miners were disarmed, put on a train, and taken to a bucolic area where the next day a group of mounted men rode and, without warning, fired at them. Although local history calls this the "Mission Massacre," no proof emerged that anyone was killed. But at least seventeen were wounded, while others ran for cover. Only fifteen of the original hundred and thirty men boarded a rescue boat, while most of the others walked thirty miles over the mountains to Coeur d'Alene; one man supposedly went all the way to Spokane, Washington (because it is a Pacific Coast seaport it sounds much further away than its thirty-three or so mile distance from Coeur d'Alene). Although there are numerous conflicting accounts of the 11 July fighting, most of them agree that a union miner was shot at, an ineffective rifle battle occurred at the Frisco mill, the miners made an abortive attempt to dynamite this mill, it was later successfully dynamited with explosives that slid down a flume, and there was a deadly rifle battle at the Gem mill. Before the day was over several men were killed and a number wounded, including George Pettibone, who devised the flume dynamiting method. On 12 July the owners persuaded the governor of Idaho to declare martial law and to ask President Benjamin Harrison to send in the National Guard to suppress the uprising and restore order, which he did; the troops arrived two days later. On 15 July union officers, union members, and sympathizers were arrested and nonunion workers returned to the mines under military protection.[6]

The Coeur d'Alene labor confrontation of 1899 was the result of mining companies lowering miners' wages, hiring detectives to infiltrate the union, and regularly firing miners who held union cards. Between 1892 and 1899 there were ferocious, sometimes fatal retaliations from both sides. An early victim was John Kneebone, a witness for the prosecution in 1892, who returned in 1894 and was murdered. The grand jury investigating this found no one who could provide clues to the killer's identity. People who left the area but did not return were "kneeboned," as locals called it. In 1899 mining companies paid a differential rate of $2.50 and $3.00. Management justified these wages on the basis that the mines were dry, which eliminated the need to buy expensive rubber clothing. The cost of boarding sank to a dollar a week. Managers of other mines testified to the United States Industrial Commission that a miner was better off under lower wages there than in higher paying mines. To the union, nonunion mines threatened the district's wage scale and the union shop. The company had spotters and detectives ferreting out union men in other mines and having them fired. On 23 April a committee from the local Wardner union (30-odd miles from Coeur d'Alene) met with the mine manager and demanded a $3.50 uniform wage and union recognition, with the penalty of a strike to accomplish this. For several days the company had discharged union employees, but management, pressured, agreed to a wage increase of fifty cents a day—in a differential of $3.00–$3.50. But it demanded that its employees must choose between employment and union membership; they could not have both. Within a day, fifty men quit. On 26 April a crowd of armed union men stopped nonunion men from working in a nearby concentrator and seized the aerial tramway. They told the nonunion men that they could not continue to work in the mines unless they worked under the protection of soldiers. Three days later a calamitous event occurred. Union workers took over a railroad train, drove it to Wardner and, at the mine there, detonated eighty fifty-pound boxes of dynamite, which as one would imagine did a great deal of damage, including the destruction of a valuable machine. On 4 May federal troops arrived at Coeur d'Alene and arrested several union members.[7]

That night the governor of Idaho telegraphed President William McKinley that since the legislature was not in session and therefore impossible to convene, he requested the president to call out "the military forces of the United States to suppress insurrection" in the county. The action was necessary because "all of the available Idaho National Guard volunteered for service in the Philippines, and said county is in a state of insurrection." Although five hundred troops would be needed, "smaller detachments should be ordered in as rapidly as possible." President McKinley promptly ordered troops to go there. When they arrived on 2 May arrests had begun, for the governor's representative, Bartlett Sinclair, believed that everyone in the area had a criminal history and that all the men should be arrested. The soldiers searched every house and if no one answered they broke down the door. At Sinclair's orders they arrested virtually all the men: miners, bartenders, a doctor, a preacher, the postmaster, cooks and waiters, diners at their tables. American Army troops followed miners into Montana, arrested them and returned them to Idaho—ignoring jurisdictional or extradition laws. One victim was a Montana citizen with no connection to the Idaho events. For union members it was 1892 redux, and some of them escaped before the troops arrived; all who remained were arrested and detained despite no charges having been filed against them. Because they knew of the imminent illegal mob action but did not try to prevent it, the county sheriff and county commissioner were given the chance to resign, but they refused; they were removed from office in impeachment proceedings. Despite the opposition of mine owners, who wanted work to start again, Sinclair instituted a work permit system that required miners to sign a statement denying participation in the crimes of 29 April and membership in any organization that incited or approved these crimes. In a few years Colorado officials adopted this permit system under similar circumstances. The 1899 actions of the governor and Sinclair destroyed the power of the Western Federation of Miners in Idaho.[8]

The twentieth century began with a change. Anthracite coal, which burns cleaner than bituminous, was a monopoly of mine owners, railroads, and bankers. To keep wages low, owners brought in immigrants from eastern and southern Europe, whose languages and customs differed from each other and from those of Americans. Although the United Mine Workers had 8000 members, 147,000 men went on strike in May 1902. Owners underestimated the workers' militancy; the union, the owners' opposition to it. Owners refused to negotiate. Ironically, the non-English speaking workers, brought in to break the union, supported it. Maintenance crews (engineers, firemen, pump men) joined strikers. Injecting

God into the dispute, an industry spokesman praised "'Christian men to whom God in His infinite wisdom has given the control of the property interests of the country,'" rather than labor agitators, to protect the interests of miners. As winter neared, with the prospect of shortages and widespread riots, progressive President Theodore Roosevelt, who believed capital and labor had public responsibilities, called a meeting on 3 October to discuss the problem—unlike Grover Cleveland, who eight years earlier had sent the army to stop a railroad strike in Illinois. Since the meeting implied recognition of the UMW, the union's head was conciliatory. Roosevelt blamed the intransigent owners for rejecting mediation. The mine workers almost unanimously voted not to return to work until the owners made concessions. On 9 October the banker J. Pierpont Morgan proposed that miners return to work while a commission studied the issues. The face-saving gimmick: industry and labor would explain differences to a commission, so that the owners would not deal directly with a union while showing the public that they would arbitrate. On 11 October, pressured by Morgan, the mine owners agreed if they could set ground rules: no negotiations with a union spokesman and a commission limited to five: a military and a mining engineer, a judge, an expert in coal business and an "eminent sociologist." The UMW balked at their effort to stack the deck. It wanted a man who understood labor, also a Roman Catholic prelate because most miners were Catholic. The owners wanted no labor man, but Roosevelt persuaded them to let him make appointments under their titles. The head of the railway conductors' union was the "eminent sociologist" and they consented to his adding a Catholic bishop. The commission split the differences. The miners wanted 20 percent salary increases; most got 10 percent. They wanted an eight-hour day; they got nine (ten was the norm). On 22 October the strike ended.[9]

1913 saw general strikes around the globe, including the United States, Belgium, the Antipodes, and Ireland. I will treat them in this order.

The 1913 strike in America that received national attention at the time (1913–1914) and that warrants our attention now, is aptly called the "Colorado Coalfield War." It concerned, as a Library of Congress research guide states, "human rights, power and money,... violence, death and destruction to tens of thousands of people and their homes." The strike ended in failure. Conditions in Colorado mines were dreadful. As an area web site states, its colliers "experienced twice the number of deaths compared to anywhere else in the world." This reflected the mine owners' indifference to safety. If nonunionized colliers complained of working conditions, “they would be fired on the spot,” and since the company provided housing, they “ended up in the street.” A miner’s workday was twelve hours for at least six days a week. Some miners had twelve-hour shifts seven days a week. Time off? Overtime pay? No such things. The mines were part of the Colorado Fuel and Iron Company (CF&I), whose principal stockholders and owners were the Rockefeller family, whose patriarch, John D. Rockefeller, had founded Standard Oil. During the 1913–1914 strike, his son, John D. Rockefeller, Jr., who ran the family’s interests, was staunchly anti-unionist and savagely fought efforts to unionize his mines. “Union colliers were fired, tarred and feathered, beaten, threatened, or rounded up and deported across state lines to be abandoned on remote stretches of prairie.” But the UMW was established in the state in 1890 and in southern Colorado a year later. The strike started on 16 September 1913 when the UMW urged its members to strike for demands that included recognition of the union, a 10 percent increase in wages (which were the lowest in the Rocky Mountain States), an eight-hour workday (a state law not complied with), the enforcement of Colorado’s mining laws (other laws not complied with) and the right to buy anything in any store, to choose any boarding house and doctor (again a law not complied with). Recall the song “Sixteen Tons,” whose famous lines “another day older and deeper in debt” and “I owe my soul to the company store” refer to the bondage of workers trapped in jobs whose stores, owned by their employers, accepted only scrip (company-printed money, in lieu of cash, for wages), which stores elsewhere did not accept. With rent in company-owned lodgings deducted from their pay, it was almost impossible for workers to save or leave. Before the miners voted whether to strike, Mother Jones herself—the seventy-six-year-old Irish-born Mary G. Harris Jones, a famous union organizer, activist, and co-founder of the IWW—spoke to them. “‘Rise up and strike,’” she cried. “‘If you are too cowardly to fight for your rights, there are enough women in the country to come in and beat hell out of the operators for you. Strike, and knock off the shackles of slavery! Strike and regain your manhood!’” The result: a unanimous yes. The majority of miners lived in company houses and had signed leases that allowed the company to evict them if they went on strike. With winter not far ahead, thousands of men and their families actually lost the roofs over their heads. Some crowded into homes of relatives or friends, or on farms and ranches. A few tried to leave Colorado to seek work elsewhere. Tens of thousands of union members who voted for the strike faced homelessness. In response, the

UMW built tent colonies in the strike zone, rented land from ranchers and other landowners, imported or bought tents, laying out colonies of canvas. When winter arrived, the already daunting situation became worse, especially when a Colorado blizzard heaped three or more feet of snow on the strikers' tents in December. When the strikers' demands were ignored, 9000 miners in Colorado went out and violence erupted.[10]

For a month, there were outbreaks of ferocity. The mining operators hired anti-union mercenaries and strikebreakers from West Virginia, says Natalie Larsen, "to harass the strikers and break the union. The detectives drove around in machine-gun equipped cars and assaulted [a] tent colony, killing a striker and a small boy." For their part, the strikers harassed scabs, who continued to work, and threatened them and their families unless they joined the strike. As conditions deteriorated, a company guard was murdered. On 28 October Colorado Governor Elias Ammon declared martial law and ordered the National Guard to go to the coalfields. With machine guns and high-powered rifles, they held off strikers. Because violence intensified and because the National Guard drained the state's money, he allowed mine operators to bring in strikebreakers. From its start to its end, the strike was exceptionally fierce. Ambushes, gunfights, and assassinations were common. Early on, residents of Ludlow (a ghost town today) welcomed state soldiers, hoping they would become neutral peacekeepers. This expectation did not last, for the National Guard moved from neutrality to favoring the CF&I. The state treasurer, a union sympathizer, distrusted the National Guard because of its role in previous strikes, when it favored mining companies. But he saw that the cost of keeping them "was bankrupting the state." The CF&I, a conglomerate, agreed to pay money for them, and Colorado's largest banks, all anti-union, helped bankroll the Guard. However, its functions aimed to be short and its tours of duty were usually only three months. By early 1914 its soldiers began to leave. Taking their place were guards, mercenaries, and gunmen hired by the CF&I. On 22 January a group of women from Trinidad (less than fifteen miles from Ludlow) marched, Thomas Andrews says, "to protest the detention of Mother Jones by National Guardsmen, who proceeded to hold her without filing formal charges." The riot that ensued symbolized "the National Guard's descent from peace-keeping neutrals to war-making partisans."[11]

On 20 April 1914 a succession of bombs exploded in the military camp. After the third bomb came retaliation. Bullets ripped through the miners' tents at Ludlow. Fighting went on during the whole day. In the evening, soldiers rode to the tent colony on horseback, with brooms dipped in kerosene, and set the tents on fire. That day in Ludlow, four men, two women, and eleven children were killed; the women and children suffocated in pits below the tents. While the fire was smoldering, striking miners in southern Colorado retaliated with weapons in what contemporaries called "the ten days' war." When news of the massacre reached the newspapers, there was—despite the coverage being marked, as Thomas Andrews says, "by sharp ideological divides"—a public outcry. In major cities across the United States, people took to the streets in protest. In the following ten days, colliers retaliated by setting fire to dozens of mine installations and dynamiting mine buildings and workings worth thousands of dollars (which would be hundreds of thousands today). During the Colorado Coalfield War, more than fifty people, including those at Ludlow, were killed. The fighting stopped when President Woodrow Wilson sent Federal troops to disarm both sides. The results? On 10 December 1914 the UMW ran out of money and called off the strike. The strikers did not get their demands, the union did not get recognition, and many striking miners were replaced.[12]

The general strike in Belgium, from 14 to 25 April 1913, which the Liberal and Socialist parties created, was not for higher wages or fewer workday hours, but for the substitution of "universal adult suffrage" for "the system of plural voting." "Universal" did not include women, for enfranchisement would extend the vote only to male workers who were not property owners. "Plural voting," then in force, was the right to cast more than one ballot. The number of strikers in this small European country of seven and a half million people rose from 300,000 at the start to 400,000 on 19 April. Except for Antwerp, a port city, transportation was not seriously affected, and neither railways nor streetcars stopped serving the public. Although the country's life "was not brought to a standstill, and although the immediate needs of the nation were supplied, yet large-scale production was completely arrested." As a result of this general strike, the prime minister agreed to appoint a commission *to discuss* amending the municipal and provincial franchises and "*might* also occupy itself by '*talking*' of the parliamentary franchise" (italics are mine). Both the socialist and labor parties considered this satisfactory. The author of an article on this subject, published three months after the strike ended, concludes that an "impartial observer" is bound to be apprehensive about the future, since "It is clear that the temptation to repeat this kind of experiment will henceforth be very strong; and we may well ask with anxiety what irreparable misfortunes such events might not bring in their train, if they were frequently repeated." Although I fail to see how this strike could be considered successful, it created enough anxieties to make the ruling classes consider discussing the issues.[13]

In New Zealand, the workers, who had been defeated in the maritime strike of 1890, suggested a compulsory arbitration system, hoping, as G.G. Hancox and J. Hight put it, "that the Government would do for them what they were unable to do for themselves." In 1894 such a law was passed "to facilitate the settlement of industrial disputes by conciliation and arbitration." It sought to end large and dangerous strikes and lockouts by establishing tribunals that would regulate labor conditions. The Arbitration Court consisted of three members: a judge and two assessors, one chosen by the industrial union of the employers, the other by that of the workers. Because the last two would tend to be biased, the judge would hold the real power. The Arbitration Court's decisions would be binding on employers, workers, and their unions, with heavy fines for breaches. The hostility of the employers gradually diminished, but when the unions realized that the Act did not grant them a large increase in wages because the court believed wages were already too high, they started to rebel against it. Between 1905 and 1913 there were ninety-eight strikes, thirty-five of them within the scope of the Act. In January 1913 the Federation of Labour and the United Labour Party held a conference that laid the basis for their union, which was partially effected, since the moderate unions considered the new party too extreme in its readiness to call a local, general, or national strike, particularly in the event of a lockout.[14]

According to Peter Clayworth, New Zealand's Great Strike of 1913, which was actually a series of strikes between mid-October 1913 and mid-January 1914, was one of the country's "most violent and disruptive industrial confrontations." It began with two small disputes and mushroomed. Its key issue "was a power struggle of militant unionists against organised employers and farmers, backed by the government." Most of these unions were affiliated with the United Federation of Labour (UFL), called by its opponents the "Red Feds," which withdrew from the country's arbitration system to directly negotiate with the New Zealand Employers' Federation and the Farmers' Union, which the prime minister fully backed to defeat the unions. The strike started with the wharf laborers' and miners' unions, later joined by unions of seamen, transport, and construction workers. It affected most port cities and coal mining areas.[15]

On 31 January 1913, say Hancox and Hight, the Waterside Workers' Union demanded higher wages, traveling allowances, and other concessions for shipwrights (ship builders). One of the small initial strikes, says Clayworth, began on 6 October when a coal mining company sacked sixteen miners, three of them union officials (to the company they were Red Feds). The miners voted to strike until they were reinstated and walked off the job until January 1914. In October a waterfront strike arose from a dispute between Wellington shipwrights and the Union Steamship Company over travel time, wages, and conditions. On 17 October, according to Hancox and Hight, the employers refused to consider these requests and stated that they would consider any stoppage of or interference with work a breach of agreement. The next day the shipwrights went on strike. While longshoremen met to discuss it, Clayworth notes, their jobs were given to others. They called a strike until they were reinstated. The ship owners formed a "defence committee" and canceled their agreement with the workers, who rejected their offer to reemploy them only if the union registered under the arbitration act or paid a bond against striking. The owners aimed to separate the longshoremen from the UFL, which they wanted to destroy, and force them back to the arbitration system. Negotiations broke down. Within a week the country's longshoremen struck in sympathy, as did coal miners.[16]

As both Clayworth's and Hancox and Hight's articles report, on 20 October the Waterside Workers' Union called a work stoppage on the 22nd to meet and consider the grievances and claims of ship workers as well as possible action. At the meeting, it was agreed to present the dispute to the UFL and officials of the Waterside Workers' Union. Since the employers were willing to let those who stopped work return to work, but not in the positions they held before the meeting, the Waterside workers considered this a lockout and a meeting of 1500 workers passed a resolution that no work would be accepted until those who had stopped work were reinstated. The shipping companies refused. On 22 October the strike or lockout of 1600 Wellington waterside workers began. The grievance of the shipwrights changed from the initial issues to the instigation of the larger strike. Acts of violence were committed. With employers and employees at loggerheads, the prime minister suggested that a Supreme Court judge arbitrate. The representatives of the workers and employers found this unacceptable. On the 24th strike supporters broke through the gates, tore down a barricade at a wharf, and "persuaded" strikebreakers to stop working. The acting commandant of New

Zealand's army, reluctant to use soldiers, persuaded the government to employ part-time volunteers in rural areas as mounted special constables, which it did. Rural men were keen to volunteer, for the strike threatened their livelihood and the socialist views of the Red Feds were at odds with their patriotic values. The special constables arrived in Wellington on the evening of 29 October. The next morning a thousand strike supporters drove them out. To intimidate them, sailors paraded with fixed bayonets and a machine gun. On 30 October mounted special and regular police charged the crowd. Allegedly, shots were fired. Similar actions occurred elsewhere. From the start, the UFL leaders were unenthusiastic about the strike, which they considered a tactical mistake that put the new union at risk because it was too soon for it to have accumulated financial resources, but they were committed to the strike because it had been decided democratically. On the 29th the troubles spread to other New Zealand cities, where watersiders struck in sympathy. Newly appointed special constables appeared in Wellington. In the four major New Zealand ports, shipping was at a standstill. In November Wellington's Defense Force paraded with rifles, bayonets, and a machine gun. The Prime Minister presided over a conference of representatives of employers and the UFL, who were at loggerheads over the principle of compulsory arbitration. Afterwards, the employers issued a manifesto refusing to negotiate with any organization not registered under the Arbitration Act. The coal miners joined the sympathy strike and other unions threatened to follow suit. Strikers and strike sympathizers assaulted special police forces, who fought back—with batons on one side, road metal on the other. The strike committee announced that it would not deal with anything under the Arbitration Act but would accept legislation empowering a Stipendiary Magistrate's Court. Although a spirit of conciliation was in the air, no plan proved acceptable to both parties. The seizure of Wellington and Auckland wharves reduced the strikers' power. Outside Auckland, few arbitrationist unions joined them. In December the Supreme Court ruled it illegal for arbitration unions to financially assist strikers from other industries. Conclusively, the strike showed many unionists the state's ability to crush strikes.[17]

On 10 November the UFL, in unambiguous terms, called for a general strike:

> In view of the gigantic conspiracy to smash organised labour, and the life and death struggle throughout New Zealand in order to preserve unionism

> against armed blacklegism, we call upon your union to make it a common cause, by refusing to work till the armed scabs leave the city. Auckland is magnificently solid. Will you follow? Labour's defeat means Labour's annihilation.

Moderate labor leaders disapproved of this action, but since fourteen unions with almost 10,000 members were on strike in Auckland, a general strike already existed there, and it involved both the Red Feds and the moderate arbitrationist unions, which were shocked by the government's level of force. The Strike Committee at Christchurch considered a general strike calamitous and Dunedin unions were lukewarm to the idea. Of fifty-three unions, four responded to the appeal. On 11 November prominent labor leaders were arrested for using language intended to cause a breach of the peace. On days that followed, two more leaders were arrested for sedition. In some cities the strike weakened; in others, business was paralyzed. In Wellington and Auckland more special forces were sworn in—over 3000 men—to preserve order and allow the shipping companies and merchants to continue business. At Christchurch it took a week for the port to reopen. Wellington wharves became busy. The same was true at other ports. At the end of the week, the strike, except for the miners, was almost broken. On 1 December Huntly coal miners refused to return to work. Six Dunedin strike leaders, arrested on the charge of intimidation, were ordered to keep the peace. Sympathetic waterside workers in Sydney, Australia, refused to handle cargo to or from New Zealand, and the Federated Seamen's Union of Australia did likewise. In New Zealand the Defense Committees of the Employers' Federation and the Farmers and Citizens condemned the UFL for having broken their agreements. The employers refused to negotiate with so hostile an organization. The president of the UFL, charged with incitement to violence, was sentenced to three months in jail.[18]

As Hancox and Hight state, the failure of New Zealand's general strike was largely due to the public's reaction against the acts of the workers, "the violent speech and extreme action of the United Federation of Labour," their non-observation of contracts, and the United Federation's pitting itself against both the employers and the community. The victory of the employers made the workers "realise, as they had not done before, the direction that a section of the labour movement has been taken during the last few years, and it has reaffirmed many of the old and commonplace lessons of strikes.... The struggle may lead them to see that the general strike... is a weapon with a dangerous recoil."[19]

Because Dublin's general strike precipitated a massive lockout (a strike-breaking tool) as a response, it is called the Dublin 1913 Lockout. In 1886 William Martin Murphy, a conservative, Catholic financier (of railroad and tram lines, and of newspapers) who paid tram workers 25 percent less than their counterparts in Belfast and Glasgow received, helped establish the Dublin Trades Council. His employees worked up to seventeen hours a day. He used fines, suspensions, and dismissals for infractions, and he encouraged informers. To him, the notion that organized workers could dictate terms of employment was abhorrent. He saw James Larkin's Irish Transport and General Workers (ITGWU) as a godless menace, says Padraig Yeates, a view shared by Dublin's middle class, the Catholic Church, business leaders, and nationalist politicians. In August Larkin thought it feasible to win union recognition by the Dublin United Tramway Company (DUTC). For six months, through sympathetic strikes (also called sympathy strikes), he had won disputes that got 20–25 percent pay raises for unskilled Dublin workers. Lack of job applicants and threats of sympathetic acts were often enough to gain concessions. He convinced "thousands of unskilled men and women, many of them illiterate and living on the breadline, not to pass pickets and accept that 'an injury to one is the concern of all.'" Employers countered with the sympathetic lockout. When tram drivers and conductors left their trolleys on 26 August at 9.40 a.m., trams moved forty minutes later, thanks to Murphy's contingency plan: inspectors and office staff, some with revolvers, replaced them—but not at night, for fear of stoning. Within days, daytime service was almost normal. Larkin relied on fewer than two hundred of the eight hundred DUTC workers, two hundred of whom had been sacked, the rest frightened into submission. As Ireland's current President Michael D. Higgins said, the Lockout was "in a city wracked with poverty, infant mortality, illness and near starvation." Yeates thinks the dispute would "have petered out but for 'Bloody Sunday,' 31 August." Kindled by the strike's failure to stop tram service, spurred by Larkin's rhetoric, workers rioted the day before. Disturbances spread to most working-class districts. On Sunday the Dublin Metropolitan Police and Royal Irish Constabulary "injured between 400 and 600 people in ferocious baton charges...." Britain's Trades Union Congress (TUC) supported the Dubliners and for seven months donated over £106,000 in money, food, fuel, and clothes. With class war in Dublin, British unionists and politicians questioned Larkin's policy. By 4 September Murphy persuaded over four hundred Dublin employers to lock out employees who refused to oppose the ITGWU. In a few weeks they locked out fifteen thousand workers, who became dependent on TUC food. Thousands more, including nonunion casual workers and the self-employed, were destitute. Unlike the sum raised by the TUC, local and Catholic Church support was paltry. The lockout affected children, whose death rate from infectious diseases rose by nearly 50 percent. Facing starvation because food ships stopped coming from England, Dubliners accepted the inevitable and returned to work. By February 1914 Murphy won. What none of the antagonists foresaw was World War I, which began six months later. Labor shortages enabled the ITGWU and other unions to recover.[20]

Shaw was not silent about events in his native city. In London in November 1913 he joined fellow socialist James Connolly, who with Larkin formed the Irish Citizen Army that month and would become a leader in the 1916 Easter Rising, in a meeting to protest the sentencing of Larkin for seditious libel. Focusing on union attempts to send children of strikers to English foster homes during the strike, which the Catholic Church stymied because living in Protestant homes would endanger the children's Catholicism, Shaw was as militant as Connolly. Shaw implored his English audience to ponder the horror of "a strike, the cessation of the weekly wage, and all that it means. Imagine what kind of men they must be who, seeing all this, thrust the children back into that starvation and misery," and "more horrible: a Christian priest doing that." Still worse was "the great Christian Church to which they belong being made the catspaw of gentlemen like Mr. Murphy." A year before, the government had prosecuted labor leader Tom Mann under the Incitement to Mutiny Act for reading a famous "Don't shoot" letter by a Liverpool worker, addressed to soldiers confronting strikers, which "was bad enough," but it required you "to talk sense to a soldier." Yet under the Sedition Act anyone who cheered the speakers on that very day could "be fined £100,000 and imprisoned for life." A government that allows charging Larkin with sedition because he said employers lived on profits shows an absence of shame almost impossible to characterize. Then came the real shocker: unless responsible men, supervised by an officer responsible to a parliamentary minister, apply force, Shaw warned, "you may as well let loose in the streets a parcel of mad dogs as a parcel of policemen."

When there are difficulties with workers, it is customary to let the police loose and do their worst. "Now, if you put the policeman on the footing of a mad dog it can only end in one way—that all respectable men will have to arm themselves." A man in the audience asked, "What with?" Shaw's reply: "arm yourselves with something that would put a decisive stop to the proceeding of the police." This "so outraged the editor of the *Daily Sketch* that... the paper called for his arrest for inciting to armed revolt."[21]

Despite his militancy on the Dublin Lockout, Shaw called general strikes "probably the most thoughtless absurdity in the whole range of Labour politics." At its mildest, a strike is "an organized annoyance. At its worst it is an act of unofficial civil war. Now, the one thing a war cannot be is general." In a week or less it would lead to starvation "and the workers would be the first to succumb." Because big strikes involve such industries as railways, which produce the effects of a general strike, they collapse. Railways feed modern civilization. Strikes that paralyze railways expose "the supposed trump card of the general strike—famine." The 1910 French railway strike collapsed in two days "and seemed to us in England to be over almost as soon as it had begun." As a way of making politicians capitulate, a general strike is stupid. As a way of forcing workers to capitulate quickly and abjectly, it is unrivaled. Shaw did not unwaveringly support smaller industrial strikes. Five years before the British General Strike of 1926, he called the right to strike "the right to commit suicide or to starve on their enemy's doorstep." A general strike would quickly collapse. In 1914, recognizing that "a trade union's main weapon was the strike," he warned that "the authorities were generally strong enough to keep order and reduce the strike to a test of endurance between the employer [and the workers], the employer having to go without profits" and the men's families having to go on insufficient food and starve. But a sectional strike can be effective, for instance, one by "waiters in a fashionable restaurant, hurting nobody but the enemy, and putting him for the moment in a corner from which he will extricate himself by any reasonable sacrifice." A strike of ladies' maids or gamekeepers "might shake the governing classes more than all the so-called general strikes of the last ten years. The 'down-napkins' strikes at restaurants were as swiftly and suddenly effective as the general strike in Sweden was futile." Shaw may allude to the 1895 strike of waitresses of the profitable Lyons tea shops for higher pay. They struck in the middle of dinner hour and publicized it as "Lyons versus the Lambs," damaging Lyons's reputation and attracting the press's attention. Lyons conceded.[22]

The year after the 1913 strikes and lockouts came World War I. The unions agreed not to strike and to accept government arbitration for the duration; the government limited profits of firms doing war work, with trade benefits going to the nation. The English historian A.J.P. Taylor called it "war socialism." In the first few months coal production increased. By March over 191,000 miners had joined the armed forces. The Miners' Federation of Great Britain demanded a 20 percent wage increase because of inflation. Agreements were reached in most areas, but in South Wales the owners offered only 10 percent, prompting a strike in 1915. Parliament immediately passed the Munitions of War Act, legislating compulsory arbitration, prohibition of strikes, and changes in wages in vital industries without consent of the Minister of Munitions. Workers in them were forbidden to leave their jobs without a "certificate of leave." The TUC leaders and the Labour Party endorsed it. When David Lloyd George became prime minister the next year, he negotiated a settlement that conceded almost all the miners demanded. Their wages rose 18½ percent.[23]

During the war, profits from coal mining increased. As Germany's coal production dwindled, higher wages became affordable in Britain. "In a conflict infamous for its lack of decisive war-winning battlefield victories," Joseph Zeller says, "it was the side best able to sustain the unrelenting need for ever more manpower and resources that was going to win." This meant crossing the sea. Britain's naval blockade was decisive. Coal generated most electricity in Germany and fueled its trade, transportation, and everyday life (cooking and heat in winter). As early as 1915 shortages caused transportation obstructions that included moving soldiers to the front. Coal could not be moved for lack of coal. With miners conscripted, Germany used underfed prisoners of war as slave labor under hazardous, inhumane conditions. Before war's end, German industry was 40 percent below its prewar level. Britain virtually monopolized steamship coal and refueling stations, devastating Germany.[24]

After the war, relations between European owners and workers became business as usual. With the return of miners to the labor force and coal not needed for war operations, prices sank. Mine owners lowered wages and increased working hours. The Soviet Revolution of 1917 both emboldened and fragmented left-wing workers as it terrified capitalists and governments, which joined to destroy unions—organizations that they considered breeding grounds for communist revolutions. Europe was in a postwar depression, as was Britain. In America the promise of Theodore Roosevelt's progressivism gave way to a reversion to the *status quo ante*.

Emblematic of the failure of general strikes in America is the Seattle General Strike of 1919, which Erik Loomis calls "the first citywide collective action in American history known as a general strike." The Pacific Northwest was a hotbed of radicalism. "Horrible working conditions in the timber industry, already radicalized immigrants from Scandinavia, activist dockers and the popularity of the Industrial Workers of the World"—the IWW, often derided as "the Wobblies," a term whose origin no one knows, but the Wobblies themselves were quick to adopt it—"among the region's thousands of transient workers made Seattle a fertile center of radical thought." For five days shipbuilders, dock workers, even barbers, telephone operators, garment makers, and streetcar conductors did not go to work. Local unionists joined shipyard workers, who demanded higher pay because of inflation. Tens of thousands more stopped working. Shops, offices, and factories closed. A general strike, uncommon in the United States, paralyzed the region's economy. Union members did more than walk off their jobs. They helped provide Seattle with social services, including health care, food (community kitchens served up to 30,000 meals a day), neighborhood milk distribution, and garbage collection. But there were limits to social solidarity: the unions leading the strike had no Black and Asian workers or women, and while unions of Japanese immigrants joined the walkout, they had no vote on strike issues. Leading the opposition, Seattle's mayor persuaded President Woodrow Wilson to call out the National Guard and publicized a red scare. The strike was crushed.[25] Other large strikes in America and Europe met the same end.

Proponents of general strikes and communism often prioritize ideological purity or uplift over reality. An article on the failed French railway strikes of 1920 claims they showed that "a nascent Communist party could build" on them. Belittling the view that they failed "because they did not precipitate the social or political revolution that contemporaries expected, desired, or feared," it stresses "the educative role" of a strike in group and individual consciousness; it blames "organizational deficiencies" for the defeat of a strike that most workers did not want. Jointly, companies' and government's actions crushed the general strike after one day. To recoup losses, owners dismissed strikers and ignored the agreement that prohibited them from doing this. Shaw sided with the majority of French union members: the strike should not have occurred. Since majorities determine elections, we think "every question that is put to the vote must be settled in the same way." At times a majority of one is conclusive. "But sometimes nothing short of virtual unanimity is of any use." Strikes require the largest majorities for affirmative settlement. "If a strike vote were taken of the half million British miners, and a quarter of a million plus one were for striking, and a quarter of a million minus one against it, any leader who attempted to call the miners out on the ground that there was a majority for the strike would have to be sent straight to Bedlam." A general strike with roughly half the members against it is absurd, yet something similar happened in France. Only success could vindicate its leaders. It failed. "Moral: majorities cannot do what they like; and don't you forget it."[26]

Notes

1. Bernard Shaw, "The Dictatorship of the Proletariat," *The Labour Monthly*, October 1921, reprinted in *Practical Politics*, ed. Lloyd J. Hubenka (Lincoln: University of Nebraska Press, 1976), p. 170.
2. Patrick Grubbs, "General Trades Union Strike (1835)," *Encyclopedia of Greater Philadelphia*, https://philadelphiaencyclopedia.org/archive/general-trades-union-strike-1835/.
3. "The Great Railroad Strike," *Digital History*, https://www.digitalhistory.uh.edu/disp_textbook.cfm?smtID=2&psid=3189; Harry Cannon, "Use of Federal Troops in Labor Disputes," *Monthly Labor Review*, 53.3 (September 1941): 561–66, https://www.jstor.org/stable/41816623?seq=1#metadata_info_tab_contents.
4. Jörg Rössel, "Industrial Structure, Union Strategy, and Strike Activity in American Bituminous Coal Mining, 1881–1894," *Social Science History*, 26.1 (Spring, 2002): 6–7, https://www.jstor.org/stable/40267769.
5. "Coeur d'Alene Mining Insurrection: Topics in Chronicling America," *Library of Congress Research Guides*, https://guides.loc.gov/chronicling-america-coeur-mining.
6. *Coeur d'Alene Miners' Dispute (1892–1899)*, http://www.3rd1000.com/history3/events/cdamines/1892-1899.htm; "Coeur d'Alene Mining Insurrection: Topics in Chronicling America," *Library of Congress Research Guides*, https://guides.loc.gov/chronicling-america-coeur-mining.

7. *Coeur d'Alene Miners' Dispute (1892–1899)*, http://www.3rd1000.com/history3/events/cdamines/1892-1899.htm; "Coeur d'Alene Mining Insurrection: Topics in Chronicling America"; Ralph Wetmur, "The Coeur d 'Alene Mines strike of 1899," 25 March 2005, reprinted from the *Coeur d Álene Press*, Centennial Edition, Section 5, p. 2, 1963, https://ruralnorthwest.com/artman/publish/article_4805.shtml.
8. *Coeur d'Alene Miners' Dispute (1892–1899)*, http://www.3rd1000.com/history3/events/cdamines/1892-1899.htm; Ralph Wetmur, "The Coeur d 'Alene Mines strike of 1899," 25 March 2005, reprinted from the *Coeur d Álene Press*, Centennial Edition, Section 5, p. 2, 1963.
9. Jonathan Grossman, "The Coal Strike of 1902: Turning Point in U.S. Policy," *U.S. Department of Labor*, reprinted from *Monthly Labor Review*, June 1974, https://www.dol.gov/general/aboutdol/history/coalstrike; Dan Bryan, "Teddy Roosevelt and the Coal Strike of 1902: A New Era in Labor and Government," *American History USA*, 8 February 2015, https://www.americanhistoryusa.com/teddy-roosevelt-coal-strike-of-1902/.
10. "Colorado Coalfield War: Topics in Chronicling America," *Library of Congress Research Guides*, https://guides.loc.gov/chronicling-america-colorado-coalfield-war; "The Ludlow Massacre and the Colorado Coalfield War," *Spanish Peaks Country*, https://spanishpeakscountry.com/the-ludlow-massacre-and-the-colorado-coalfield-war/; "United Mine Workers of America," *Colorado Encyclopedia*, https://coloradoencyclopedia.org/article/united-mine-workers-america; Thomas Andrews, "The Colorado Coalfield War of 1913–'14," *NIE* [Newspapers in Education], *Online*, pp. 6, 9–10, 27, https://nieonline.com/coloradonie/downloads/ludlow/educators_ludlow_resource_set.pdf; "The Ludlow Massacre and the Colorado Coalfield War," *Spanish Peaks Country*, https://spanishpeakscountry.com/the-ludlow-massacre-and-the-colorado-coalfield-war/.
11. Natalie Larsen, "The Colorado Coalfield Strike of 1913–1914," *Intermountain Histories*, 29 May 2019, https://www.intermountainhistories.org/items/show/219; Colorado Coalfield War: Topics in Chronicling America," *Library of Congress Research Guides*, https://guides.loc.gov/chronicling-america-colorado-coalfield-war; Thomas Andrews, "The Colorado Coalfield War of 1913–'14," *NIE* [Newspapers in Education], *Online*, pp. 33, 35.
12. "The Ludlow Massacre and the Colorado Coalfield War," *Spanish Peaks Country*, https://spanishpeakscountry.com/the-ludlow-massacre-and-the-colorado-coalfield-war/; Thomas Andrews, "The Colorado Coalfield War of 1913–'14," *NIE* [Newspapers in Education], *Online*, pp. 42, 47.

13. E. Mahaim, "The General Strike in Belgium," *Economic Journal*, 23.90 (June 1913): 294–97, https://www.jstor.org/stable/2222161?seq=1#metadata_info_tab_contents.
14. G.G. Hancox and J. Hight, "The Labour Movement and the Strike of 1913 in New Zealand," *The Economic Journal*, 24.94 (June 1914): 180–85, https://www.jstor.org/stable/2222419?origin=crossref&seq=1#metadata_info_tab_contents.
15. Peter Clayworth, "The 1913 Great Strike," *New Zealand History*, pp. 1–2, https://nzhistory.govt.nz/politics/1913-great-strike.
16. G.G. Hancox and J. Hight, "The Labour Movement and the Strike of 1913 in New Zealand," *The Economic Journal*, 24.94 (June 1914): 186–91, https://www.jstor.org/stable/2222419?origin=crossref&seq=1#metadata_info_tab_contents; Peter Clayworth, "The 1913 Great Strike," *New Zealand History*, pp. 3–4, https://nzhistory.govt.nz/politics/1913-great-strike.
17. Peter Clayworth, "The 1913 Great Strike," *New Zealand History*, pp. 3–4, G.G. Hancox and J. Hight, "The Labour Movement and the Strike of 1913 in New Zealand," *The Economic Journal*, 24.94 (June 1914): 186–91, https://www.jstor.org/stable/2222419?origin=crossref&seq=1#metadata_info_tab_contents.
18. G.G. Hancox and J. Hight, "The Labour Movement and the Strike of 1913 in New Zealand," *The Economic Journal*, 24.94 (June 1914): 191–96, Peter Clayworth, "The 1913 Great Strike," *New Zealand History*, p. 7, https://nzhistory.govt.nz/politics/1913-great-strike, https://www.jstor.org/stable/2222419?origin=crossref&seq=1#metadata_info_tab_contents
19. G.G. Hancox and J. Hight, "The Labour Movement and the Strike of 1913 in New Zealand," *The Economic Journal*, 24.94 (June 1914): 201–2.
20. Padraig Yeates, "The Dublin 1913 Lockout," *History of Ireland*, https://www.historyireland.com/20th-century-contemporary-history/the-dublin-1913-lockout/; President Michael D. Higgins, "The Lockout of 1913," lecture on RTÉ on 18 June 2013, *Irish Times*, 11 September 2013, https://www.irishtimes.com/culture/heritage/the-lockout-of-1913-1.1522296.
21. George Bernard Shaw, "Mad Dogs in Uniform," *The Matter with Ireland*, 2nd ed., ed. Dan H. Laurence and David H. Greene (Gainesville, FL: University Press of Florida, 2001), pp. 95–97; "1912: The Syndicalist Trials" (the letter was originally published in *The Syndicalist*, January 1912), https://libcom.org/files/1912%20The%20syndicalist%20trials.pdf.

22. G. Bernard Shaw, "The General Strike: An Imaginary Correspondence," *The New Statesman*, 1.3 (26 April 1913): 74–75; Bernard Shaw, "Redistribution of Income," lectures for the Fabian Society, 1914, p. 255; Bernard Shaw, "The Dictatorship of the Proletariat," *The Labour Monthly*, October 1921, reprinted in *Practical Politics*, p. 170; T. Farrell, "Roaring Trade: A History of J. Lyons (1894–1945)," *Let's Look Again*, 19 September 2014, http://letslookagain.com/2014/09/the-rise-and-demise-of-the-j-lyons-empire/; Brenda Assael, *The London Restaurant*, 1840–1914 (Oxford: Oxford University Press, 2018), p. 120.
23. "The Coal Industry and the First World War," *Spartacus Educational*, https://spartacus-educational.com/CoalFWW.htm.
24. Joseph Zeller, "Coal: A Significant Factor in Germany's Defeat in World War I," *Canadian Military History*, 27.1 (2018): 2, 4, 6–7, 9, 13–14, 19–21, https://scholars.wlu.ca/cgi/viewcontent.cgi?article=1918&context=cmh.
25. Erik Loomis, "Shutting It All Down: The Power of General Strikes in U.S. History," *In These Times*, 2 November 2011, https://inthesetimes.com/article/shutting-it-all-down-the-power-of-general-strikes-in-u-s-history; "Theory #4—'Wobbly' as a Pejorative Slur by the Employer Class," *Industrial Workers of the World a Union for All Workers*, https://archive.iww.org/history/icons/wobbly/4/; Mark Engler, "Reviving the General Strike," *The Nation*, 1 September 2019, https://www.thenation.com/article/archive/general-strike-labor-day/.
26. Adrian Jones, "The French Railway Strikes of January–May 1920: New Syndicalist Ideas and Emergent Communism," *French Historical Studies*, 12.4 (Autumn, 1982), pp. 508–40, https://www.jstor.org/stable/286423; Bernard Shaw, "A Strike That Should Never Have Taken Place," *Labour Research Department Monthly Circular*, n.s. 6 (June 1920): 82–83.

CHAPTER 5

The British General Strike of 1926

Abstract Britain's General Strike of 1926 lasted nine days. Although the huge majority of workers—unionized coal miners, plus other union and nonunion members and the public, supported it, as unions other than that of the mineworkers called sympathetic or sympathy strikes—the strikers lost and wound up worse than they were before they struck. This chapter explores its background, the desire for nationalized coal mining, the adamant hostility of the Conservative government toward the strikers (including propaganda and outright lies, plus the use of the military and police forces), lockouts by owners, efforts to break the strike (including denying or limiting unions the means of communicating to the public, scabbing by the middle and upper classes) and union fecklessness in contrast to worker solidarity. After a day-by-day account of the strike, the chapter examines its results and aftermath.

Keywords British General Strike of 1926 · Lockout · Unions · Coal miners · Sympathetic or sympathy strikes · Wages and working conditions · Unemployment · George Bernard Shaw · The communist menace · Nationalization · Winston Churchill · Propaganda

B. F. Dukore, *Unions, Strikes, Shaw*,
Bernard Shaw and His Contemporaries,
https://doi.org/10.1007/978-3-030-99131-9_5

The General Strike of 1926, Britain's only such strike, began a minute before midnight on 3 May and ended at noon on 12 May—nine days that were what Keith Laybourn calls "the only occasion on which the vast majority of the organized working class have given their industrial, financial and moral support to a group of workers for more than a day" and the only one that "divided the nation so sharply along class lines or produced so much bitterness." Between one and a half and one and three-quarter million workers, mainly in "industries such as transport, electricity, building and gas," stopped work to support one million coal miners "locked out on 30 April for refusing to accept lower wages once the subsidy to the coal industry which had been agreed on 31 July 1925, 'Red Friday,' ran out." On 1 May (May Day, which many countries celebrate, including the U.K., but seldom in the U.S., in honor of workers) the TUC agreed to support them and gave a committee power to try to settle the General Strike and reopen negotiations between miners and mine owners to prevent wage reductions and increased workday hours.[1] The roots of this strike warrant examination. As mentioned earlier, the consideration of Britain's General Strike here virtually excludes Shaw's observations and assessments, which form the subject of Chapter 6. What Shaw said of it while it was going on was uncharacteristically little, and it will be dealt with in the following chapter.

After World War I ended in 1918, says Anne Perkins, "a bewildering number and variety of strikes by workers responding to inflation" soured the peace. Between 1919 and 1921 three times more working days were lost than in prewar years. After the Russian Revolution of 1917 many Britons thought that revolution was a sign of the times in their own country. A strike in Glasgow provoked riots that English troops and tanks put down when strikers used bricks, bottles, and iron bars; railway workers, dockers, and miners engaged in industrial disputes. In wartime the government controlled coal, pooling its output and income. Nationalization, an objective of the Labour Party, seemed logical. In 1919 almost a million miners in three thousand mines "put state ownership of the pits at the top of a list of demands that also included a six-hour working day and a 30 per cent pay rise." Miners were "victims of an unjust system of ownership that produced poverty wages and intolerable living conditions," which entitled them to support from other trade unions. The Triple Alliance (miners, dockers and railwaymen), begun in 1914, was on hold during the war. In 1920 the idea of united action revived. In his 1926 book on the General Strike, R. Page Arnot, a co-founder of the British Communist Party, points out that the Emergency Powers Act had been presciently passed, enabling two or three people plus the king to declare a state of emergency that created new types of offenses, with penalties. Clause 1: "If at any time it appears to His Majesty that any action has been taken or is immediately threatened by any persons or body of persons" which might interfere with "the supply and distribution of food, water, fuel, or light, or with the means of locomotion," and deprive much of the community with "the essentials of life," the king may proclaim a state of emergency.[2]

Initially, postwar prosperity and government control of the coal industry averted conflict. When export prices for British coal soared, the government allowed wage increases. In 1920 dockers and railwaymen, invoking the Triple Alliance, wanted the same. A temporary settlement was reached. When it expired in March 1921, profitability in coal had fallen. The government shed its wartime responsibilities for coal and railways. Instead of forthrightly addressing a key problem of the industry, which a twenty-first-century reporter calls fundamental, that "there were... too many pits—many of them uneconomic," mine owners resorted to their formula of lower wages and longer hours. Miners rejected these measures. On 1 April the owners began a lockout. As Perkins says, the miners fought "pay cuts of up to 50 per cent in areas where profitability was in sharp decline" and supported the nationalization of the industry that the government had instituted in wartime, which included the same wages for all, a national profits pool to support unprofitable pits and a national salaries board. The miners called on dockers and railwaymen to join a strike on 12 April. A state of emergency was declared with offers to subsidize coal prices for a limited time and to negotiate. On "Black Friday," 15 April 1921, when railway and transport workers' unions voted against a sympathetic strike, alliance leaders called off a general strike pending negotiations. The war "changed everything—and nothing. The distribution of income and opportunity remained grotesquely disproportionate." Statistics foreshadow those of today, some of which inflate them. Then, a fourth of the people had three fourths of the money; a tenth had 42 percent of the income; of these, 1.5 percent had over a fifth. "Only one child in ten at elementary school went on to secondary education. Less than one in a hundred from elementary school went on to a university." In the previous decade "a new, elastic middle class"— "from clerks to clerics, drapers and bank managers to professors and lawyers"—became "an influential political constituency." Some two hundred thousand of them moved from the inner city to the suburbs, isolated from their former working-class neighbors, of whose conditions they became ignorant. Not rich or poor, they behaved correctly and strove to improve themselves. Politically, they were allies of the wealthy.[3]

Four days before the 1924 general election, the *Daily Mail* published a letter, which forty years later was proved to be a forgery, from Grigori Zinoviev, head of the Communist International, about spreading the revolution to Britain. It claimed that Labour Minister Ramsay MacDonald wanted to help the revolution by provoking communist mutiny in the British armed forces. While anyone who read the *Daily Worker*, the Communist Party's newspaper, knew that Moscow had written off Britain's Labour Party as bourgeois, the letter helped Conservative Stanley Baldwin win by a landslide. After former liberals helped vote conservatives into Parliament, unemployment rose and wages fell.[4]

In 1923 France occupied German coalfields in the Ruhr—a consequence of the Treaty of Versailles, which forced Germany, financially drained by the war, to pay reparations for damages to France during World War I. A portion of Germany's debt went to France from German coal. One effect of French control of the Ruhr, which lasted for two years, was to remove German coal from the world market, which created higher prices for exported British coal. British miners recouped some of the pay cuts of 1921. In 1924 the mine owners agreed to restore the wartime minimum wage, but when the new terms kicked in, the resumption of German exports reduced the demand for British coal. With Britain's return to the gold standard in 1925 (advocated by Winston Churchill in 1924), the pound reflated, profits dropped (since it cost other countries more for British coal, they bought German coal). On 30 June mine owners cut wages, ended the minimum wage, and secured profits (a minimum of 13 percent) no matter how low wages fell. At the end of July, they announced that their agreement to pay the standard wage would end, meaning another pay cut—for some, 50 percent; owners said this might improve if miners increased workday shifts from seven hours to eight. The miners refused. The owners claimed their losses were a million pounds per month. To the contrary, the miners argued; their profits between 1921 and 1925 were close to 58½ million pounds, whereas the average shift worker earned between 9s 4d and 12s 8d a day. The TUC intervened: if there were a strike, unions would block the movement of coal. The Triple Alliance—expanded to engineering, electrical, shipyard, and iron and steel workers, and renamed the Industrial

Alliance—tried to ensure unified action. On 23 July the miners and the TUC prepared an embargo on coal. Its representatives met the prime minister. "Not a minute on the day, not a penny off the pay," said the miners in chorus, rejecting lower wages and longer shifts. On the 30th the TUC triggered the embargo. Prime Minister Baldwin capitulated, offering a subsidy until 1 May 1926 to meet the difference between owners and miners until a new commission reported. Lockout and strike were suspended. Ignoring what might happen when the subsidy ended, says Arnot, the unions hailed this as Red Friday, to block out Black Friday. Baldwin's capitulation outraged the press. Actually, said Kingsley Martin, who was editor of the *New Statesman* from 1930 to 1960, "Churchill and other militants in the cabinet were eager for the strike, knowing that they had built a national organization in the six months' grace won by the subsidy to the mining industry." How did Martin know this? Churchill had told him. In the same conversation, Churchill had called the coal commission's report a "'useless document'" and had said the subsidy was granted to help the government smash the unions unless the miners gave way.[5]

In the event of a general strike, the TUC General Council prepared only a vague strategy. It broadened grievances in matters like pay cuts in other industries, for the gold standard threatened every worker's wages. When the Post Office intercepted and leaked the strategy, parts of it alarmed the public, as the government intended; for instance, strike leaders "'*must assume actual military war* [original emphasis] to be the ultimate result of a prolonged struggle'" that "'will lead *to the final conflict and the overthrow of capitalism* [emphasis added in pencil in 1925],'" and an "early aim should be to cut off the bourgeoisie from food and other supplies." The government wanted the public to see the strike as a national threat. Fears of revolution dominated the press. MI5 (Military Intelligence, Section 5) kept communists under surveillance and made it seem that Moscow supported the revolution in Britain. MI5 supposedly had documents suggesting the Communist Party was funded by £98,764 a year—which, unlike the usual rounding-up or down of a figure, gave it the appearance of authenticity. As Perkins observes, the communists encouraged this depiction of a strength they did not have. Churchill drew connections to the Labour Party: "'Behind Socialism stands Communism. Behind Communism, Moscow, that dark sinister evil power,' he thundered, 'a band of cosmopolitan conspirators.'"[6] Today they might be called "elitist conspirators."

The government did not approve the findings of the coal commission, chaired by Sir Herbert Samuel. This commission faulted the subsidy. Instead of spending £10 million, the government spent £23 million. Almost 75 percent of coal mined in the last quarter of 1925 cost more than it could sell for. The commission asked why the working day should expand to eight hours when there was an oversupply of coal and recommended that the government should fund reorganization, pit closures, and amalgamations, agree to a national minimum wage and profit-sharing, and also finance investment. The mine owners objected to everything the commission questioned and recommended. The miners rejected a short-term pay cut until reorganization made the industry profitable. National sympathy was with them, but newspapers drummed threats of communist revolution into the public mind. Mine owners did not budge. Two hundred thousand miners were jobless. The choice was a strike or prolonged unemployment. The TUC called for a conference of union executives on 29 April to decide on whether to approve a general strike. On the 30th King George V proclaimed a state of emergency effective the next day. A leading article in the *Daily Mail*, 3 May 1926, put the case for government support of mine owners: "'A general strike is not an industrial dispute. It is a revolutionary movement intended to inflict suffering upon the great mass of innocent persons in the community and thereby to put forcible constraint upon the Government." It would "subvert the rights and liberties of the people."[7]

Negotiations collapsed. At midnight on Friday lockouts by mine owners would begin. On Saturday the TUC proposed that it negotiate during the strike. Unions representing 3.6 million workers overwhelmingly agreed. The delegates unanimously approved the General Strike, to start at the end of working shifts on Monday evening, 3 May. That same evening, rather at 4 a.m. in the morning, Beatrice Webb recorded in her diary her conviction that "the capitalists of the coal-fields are so dreary and incompetent a lot... that they have been and are wholly unable to run their business with decent efficiency"; the General Strike, due to begin in a few hours, she prophesied, "will fail; the General Council may funk it and may withdraw their instructions on some apparent concession by the Government, or the men may slink back to work in a few days." The Fabians, she explained, "have always been against a General Strike"—including Shaw, whose views on this one, as I said, the next chapter discusses. Such a strike, "to compel the employers of a particular industry to yield to the men's demands," she continued, "aims at coercing the whole community and is only successful *if it does so* and in so far as it does so. Further, if it succeeded in coercing the community" it would mean that a militant minority would starve the majority into submitting to their will, which "would be the end of democracy, industrial as well as political." Accurately, she predicted, "When the million or so strikers have spent their money they will drift back to work and no one will be any the better and many will be a great deal poorer and everybody will be cross." Its futility will be clear to everyone, particularly the "Trade Unionists who find their funds exhausted and many of their most able members victimized by being permanently displaced by patriotic blacklegs! There will be not only an excuse for but a justification of victimization on a considerable scale."[8]

With almost a million workers unemployed, says Margaret Morris, the government tried "to recruit them as strikebreakers"—with little success, despite their poverty, for "the traditional abhorrence of blacklegging was generally too deeply rooted for such pressure to succeed." Government preparations for the strike were better than those of the unions, which Patrick Renshaw calls mostly improvised. From Day 1, 4 May, Perkins says, "The miners knew they had the backing of the trade union movement, the owners the backing of the government." "'No trains of any kind must be worked by our members,'" said the National Union of Railwaymen. The Great Western Railway's manager told employees not to break their contracts lest their livelihoods be impacted. Union leaders feared that violence on picket lines might create justification for sending in troops. On 4 May city residents "woke up to silence": no noise from buses, trains, or building sites. No trams or buses left depots. Hardly a train ran. "The solidarity surprised everyone, including the TUC." Booking-office clerks, signalmen, and stationmasters joined the strikers. Some sixteen million people trying to get to work with no public transportation caused chaos. Pedestrians, bicycles, cars, horse-drawn carts, and motorized coaches and buses filled the roads. Private auto drivers gave lifts to pedestrians. The response of union members exceeded TUC expectations. So did that of volunteers—to the relief of less bellicose government members, who did not want soldiers called in. Recruitment centers had long queues. The upper classes registered at their clubs to staff canteens and to become special constables. What the volunteers achieved was dubious. Many who hoped to drive trains learned that it took days of training to acquire even rudimentary skills, and railway companies realized this when locomotives stopped on hills and stalled in tunnels. Anti-union professors threatened not to support students' degrees if they did not volunteer. Volunteers tried to help the public. Strikers and their families saw them as strikebreakers, scabs, blacklegs. As Rachelle Saltzman finds, upper-class volunteers transformed a working-class revolt "into a nine-day May festival" with larks, rags, and fancy dress—traditional university and society play genres to raise charity funds. Some students and young executives wore workers' costumes as truck drivers and bus conductors, and they threw strike parties; society women offered rides to pedestrians, became telephone operators, and served tea to volunteers. To the working classes they were play-acting, diverting attention from strike issues, and helping the government break the strike to protect business interests. The workers thought they were bad at the jobs they undertook—an elite with "liberty to do things that ordinary people would be told they were hooligans if they did." The General Strike exposed the class-based meanings of duty and service. The government and most of the upper and middle classes saw the volunteers as serving the public good, but the working class saw them as serving their class interests against those of the real workers.[9]

On Day 2 newssheets reassured people that commuters were successfully going to and from work. Information was controversial. The four-year-old government-run BBC was in a hard position because the government did not want Labour politicians or strikers to air views favoring the strike. Their voices were absent from radio. The *British Gazette*, first printed on Day 1, was Churchill's voice. Its first editorial stated its goal in racist terms: "'to prevent this great nation being reduced to the level of African natives dependent only on the rumours'" of an unconstitutional strike. On Day 3 the *Gazette* told the public, "'Constitutional Government is being attacked.... The General Strike is a challenge to Parliament and is the road to anarchy and ruin.'" Clifford Sharp, who had been the first editor of the *New Statesman* in 1913, called the *Gazette* pure propaganda and untruthful. In Parliament Churchill said he had "no use in wartime for truth and impartiality." He wanted readers to consider the strike a constitutional, not an industrial fight, and to regard the unions as threats to liberty. To the commercial press, "the only form of literature which most people find time to read," as Kingsley Martin put it, ideas do not sell papers. The press framed the strike as the Soviet Union's challenge to British freedom. But the General Strike had no revolutionary aim; its goal was to help the miners. In fact, the TUC and the Labour Party refused to let the Communist Party join them. The press claimed the TUC opposed government and Parliament. Only *The Times* and the *Manchester Guardian* gave non-hysterical news. Sir Herbert Samuel, in Italy, read misrepresentations of his commission, which had tried to avert a general strike. On May 6th he returned to England, where he arranged for an auto racing champion to drive him from Dover to London, since railwaymen were on strike. He hoped that his report would be a basis for a settlement. Subsidy would continue for a fortnight to allow negotiations arbitrated by a coal commission—but not until the General Strike was withdrawn. It was illegal, the government said, which meant that every railwayman on strike was in disregard of his employment contract and could be sued (Note 9).

Day 4 brought news and assertions from the previous night. Liverpool and Ipswich had riots; mobs in Glasgow threw stones at tram sheds that housed students ready to drive trolleys, shops, and liquor stores were looted. In Hull the Royal Navy had sailors ready to break up mobs, and mounted police reportedly charged thousands in the City Square. In York unemployment by non-strikers quadrupled. Officials hinted at civil war. The government assumed powers to make raids to search for seditious matter and did so at Communist Party headquarters. The *British Gazette* denounced the TUC as trying to starve Britain into submission. Churchill stopped the supply of paper and printer's ink to newspapers, especially the *British Worker*, which the TUC published to counter anti-strike propaganda. For him the strike was a war between the government and unions. Samuel met with TUC negotiators, reiterating that his commission had advocated national wage rates, which the mine owners had opposed, and that he had resisted a coal cartel that would lower wages (Note 11).

By Day 5 the army was camped in Hyde Park. Over a hundred trucks, escorted by armored cars with soldiers in battle gear, drove to the docks, which volunteers reopened. City councils called workers to return to work; few responded. Police dispersed strikers surrounding trams. In Plymouth violence erupted. Churchill overstated and fabricated: "'food stocks are becoming depleted throughout London, but on the other hand the first food convoy has been successfully run up from the docks.'" A call went out for volunteer police to help the 25,000-man constabulary reserves and the emergency constables. Their wages—five shillings for a constable, ten for a commander—were higher than wages for miners before their pay cuts. Since the government would not meet with the TUC even privately, Samuel issued a public letter that the TUC would welcome a meeting. By going public on this, he aimed to make the government responsible for rejection. Despite the government's giving the impression of armed insurrection that had to be combatted, Patrick Renshaw reminds us, "There were no deaths during the strike" and the four thousand arrests "represented a negligible fraction of the total number of strikers."[10]

Day 6 reported Saturday night violence, rumors of imminent arrests, and signs of military activity. Religious leaders differed. The City Temple minister declared, "There is no attack on the constitution. It is impossible to witness the remarkable order on both sides and believe that we are in the grip of reckless revolutionaries." But a Brixton vicar scabbed as an engine driver before his church service and a Catholic cardinal called the strike "a sin against God." In fact, there were both violence and order during the General Strike. In the East End of London, Christopher Farman relates, when strikers thought that vehicles were carrying explosives or office workers, strikers or strike sympathizers stopped and wrecked them, and some set them on fire or pushed them into the Thames. Street battles created casualties. Working-class areas of big cities throughout Britain saw unceasing rioting. At the same time, "Tactful police behaviour and trade union restraint prevailed in most areas throughout the strike," and there were even friendly activities between the police and the people. In fact, a French observer's "incredulous comment... when he learned of the football match between strikers and the police in Plymouth was, 'The British are not a nation, they are a circus.'" One wonders what he would have said had he learned that the mayor of Lewes "put up the prize in a public billiard match between strikers and police." Even Beatrice Webb was taken aback by the football match. "A strike which begins with a football match between the police and the strikers and ends in unconditional surrender after nine days with densely-packed reconciliation services at all the chapels and churches of Great Britain attended by the strikers and their families," she later wrote in her diary, "will make the continental Socialists blaspheme." The sheer absurdity of the General Strike of 1926 has "made the Black Friday of 1921 seem to be a red-letter day of common sense. Let me add that the failure of the General Strike has shown what a *sane* people the British are," and she calls her countrymen "hopelessly good-natured and common-sensical." To Clifford Sharp, the strike smacked "more... of comic opera than of tragedy." The belligerent Churchill spoke and wrote as if the nation were in a civil war and was fighting for "King and Country." To him, everyone who questioned or criticized governmental policy was a traitor or a Bolshevik in disguise. He had no inkling that the country did not feel like this and that public emotion was neither fear nor anger but rather pity for the miners. The Archbishop of Canterbury, officially the greatest person in the kingdom after the royal family, had consulted with the leaders of all of Britain's Protestant churches and then issued a sensible appeal for peace and renewed negotiations, but the government refused to allow this appeal to be broadcast on BBC radio (the British Broadcasting Corporation was and is publicly financed and functions under a royal charter), and Churchill refused to print it in the *British Gazette*. Churchill's basis for suppressing him was that the *Gazette* had no room for everything. The King let it become known that he was not pleased.[11]

As week 2 approached, no solution was apparent. Legal penalties and loss of jobs and pensions loomed. Strike pay depleted union funds. The *British Worker* asked those who were working to donate five shillings a week to strikers. Churchill prepared legislation outlawing sympathy strikes. The most crucial anti-strike propaganda was that public transport and railroads were functioning. This, he knew, would make people's lives seem normal, and disruption of railway service would symbolize organized labor's power. Daily reports promised rail service by volunteers and claimed that blacklegs had restarted trains or would soon do so. At the end of the first week, the BBC suggested that railwaymen were returning to work (post-strike statistics showed that only 3 percent of them did). The purpose of BBC broadcasts of how many trains ran was to give the impression the strike was falling apart. True, volunteers were completing their training and more trains were operating, but accidents increased, including four fatalities. Railway organization was chaotic. "Competent men were stranded without trains, or with trains, but in the wrong place. Signalmen were thrown into unfamiliar boxes at short notice and unskilled volunteers were accused of causing thousands of pounds' worth of damage. Strike-breaking efforts on the trams and buses, where less skill and fewer support staff were needed, had more success." On Day 7 Labour politicians still implored the BBC to be heard.[12]

On Day 8 the *British Worker* advertised, "The General Council does NOT challenge the Constitution.... Nor is it desirous of undermining our Parliamentary institutions." TUC bulletins proclaimed the rank and file's resolve to stand firm for victory. Political tenacity against the strike increased. Efforts to break it on public transportation led to violence. After a crowd of four thousand in Brighton ignored an appeal to leave, the chief constable had police on horseback force them to disperse; they galloped through the crowd, hitting and knocking down women, children, and old people. One thing was clear to the strikers: the miners would not capitulate. The only people to benefit from ending the strike would be the employers, who would exploit a weakened union, drive down pay and give jobs to nonunion workers. Samuel gave the TUC revised offers: to withdraw the strike if the government would "'arrange for a withdrawal of the lock-out notices.'" The committee accepted these, but the government refused to negotiate during the strike. Near midnight, the miners refused. On Day 9 the press, which was mostly hostile to the strike, reported that it was weakening and predicted its demise. Samuel released his final recommendations. The miners said the rank and file were enthusiastic about continuing, but the TUC delegates agreed to call off the strike. Their reason, says Laybourn, was that they saw no chance of victory. Renshaw observes, "the Labour Party was remarkably inactive during the strike" and "those who had pressed for a negotiated settlement never had any really serious chance of success." The government was not interested in negotiations; it would only accept unconditional surrender. As Perkins says, before the Prime Minister would see the negotiators in person, they had to first announce they would call off the strike. "Any lingering confusion about the degree of defeat was swiftly dispersed by the manner of the large employers when the strikers tried to return to work." To railway employers the strike's defeat was a chance to restrict union activity; the docks employers "intended to claw back recent concessions."[13]

"In the final analysis," Laybourn writes, "the General Strike revealed the real weakness of a constitutional trade union movement supporting a course of action to which it was reluctantly committed and whose consequences would have had to be measured in political as well as industrial terms." On and after 13 May, he states, the government claimed it did not concede an inch, the unions that they got enough of what they wanted. The public was bewildered and uncertain. People expected to rise the next day and take the bus to work, but with volunteers gone they found less public transportation than during the strike. They feared an uprising by disaffected unionists. The communists tried to get strikers to revolt—to no avail. Almost everyone felt betrayed. Those who struck for the miners now struck for themselves. With the General Strike off, a hundred thousand took to the streets—in some areas, more than during the strike. Employers seized the opportunity. Since employees broke their contracts by walking out, without government protection against post-strike victimization, they had to sign new contracts. The chance for unions to demonstrate strength served to confirm their weakness. No company guaranteed jobs. On the 13th came a notice from employers: "'The injury to trade is believed to be so serious that for some time full pre-strike services would not be required.'" The Great Western Railway selected whom to reemploy, and they suspended a guaranteed working week. Two days later the government proposed to end the mining strike—on terms less generous than the Samuel commission's. The miners rejected Baldwin, reiterated "Not a penny off the pay, not a minute off the day," and did not return to work. In June Baldwin—destroying credibility in government impartiality—introduced legislation suspending the seven-hour day in the mines. Fifteen years later Shaw called him "the most Conservative Prime Minister who was ever mistaken for anything else." It took six more months before the miners settled—on worse terms than those before the General Strike began. "Not until December, when winter closed in, did cold and hunger drive them back to work, in dribs and drabs, on terms of abject surrender or district pay awards; less money and longer hours had all to be conceded." Farman quotes a group of workers: "The bosses in all trades felt, in fact, that now they had the trade union movement at their feet, and all they had to do was to stamp on it."[14]

On 18 May Churchill announced in the House of Commons, as Beatrice Webb recorded in her diary on the same day, that "the General Strike will have cost the Government no more than three-quarters of a million [pounds]—a sum which the death of a couple of millionaires will pay," which she noted "puts the cap of ridicule on the heroics of the General Strike. The three million strikers will have spent some three million pounds of Trade Union money and lost another four or five in wages," returning to work "on the old conditions in wages and hours"—a forecast that overestimated the results, which as the previous paragraph shows, were much worse than she imagined.[15] She blamed the miners for plunging in with no ideas but to resist cuts in wages and lengthening workday hours; "they don't care a damn about the reorganisation of their industry and they are even hostile to the nationalisation of royalties because of their obsession about no compensation to wealthy owners" (for more on this subject, see Chapter 8). Their conduct toward the General Council was impossible, "demanding a General Strike but refusing to consult about the settlement they would accept." In addition, she reproached them for not having imagined that they themselves were taking the financial support of families of shipbuilders and ironworkers by their refusals to return to work. She also castigated labor leaders and their followers, both political and individual, who day-dreamed that social transformation would occur "in the twinkling of an eye." She did not fail to condemn herself. The visions of both sides, she admitted, were "equally fantastic and without foundation. We are all of us just good-natured stupid folk. The worst of it is that the governing class are as good-natured and stupid as the Labour Movement!".[16]

Not quite the worst of it. The governing class was neither good-natured nor stupid. One significant result of the 1926 General Strike was that the following year the conservative government passed the Trade Disputes and Trade Unions Act, which "outlawed general strikes and sympathetic strikes, and banned civil servants from joining unions affiliated" to the TUC. Because of this, the Labour Party lost a third of its dues-paying members.[17]

Notes

1. Keith Laybourn, *The General Strike of 1926* (Manchester: Manchester University Press, 1993), pp. 1–2.
2. Barrie Clement, "Class War in May 1926: Nine Days That Shook the UK," *The Independent*, 1 April 2009, https://www.independent.co.uk/news/uk/this-britain/class-war-may-1926-nine-days-shook-uk-6102058.html; Anne Perkins, *A Very British Strike 3 May–12 May 1926* (London: Macmillan, 2006), pp. 8–9, 11, 13, 16–17; R. Page Arnot, *The General Strike May 1926: Its Origin and History* (New York: Augustus M. Kelley, 1967), pp. 13–14; "Emergency Powers Act 1920," *Legislation Line*, https://www.legislationline.org/documents/id/7349.
3. Anne Perkins, *A Very British Strike 3 May–12 May 1926*, pp. 17–18, 23; Keith Laybourn, *The General Strike of 1926*, p. 19.
4. Anne Perkins, *A Very British Strike 3 May–12 May 1926*, pp. 47–548.
5. "France Occupies the Ruhr," *Inter-War Period: Causes of WW II*, https://inter-wars.weebly.com/france-occupies-the-ruhr-1923.html; Anne Perkins, *A Very British Strike 3 May–12 May 1926*, pp. 51–54; Keith Laybourn, *The General Strike of 1926*, pp. 14, 22, 66; Christopher Farman, *The General Strike May 1926* (London: Rupert Hart-Davis, 1972), p. 20; Patrick Renshaw, *The General Strike* (London: Eyre Methuen, 1975), p. 118; Kingsley Martin, *Father Figures* (London: Hutchinson, 1966), pp. 160–61.
6. Anne Perkins, *A Very British Strike 3 May–12 May 1926*, pp. 56–62, 73.

7. Anne Perkins, *A Very British Strike 3 May–12 May 1926*, pp. 81–84, 88–90; R. Page Arnot, *The General Strike May 1926*, pp. 155–56.
8. *Beatrice Webb's Diaries 1924–1932*, ed. Margaret Cole (London: Longmans, Green, 1956), pp. 89–92.
9. Margaret Morris, *The General Strike* (Harmondsworth: Penguin Books, 1976), p. 13; Patrick Renshaw, *The General Strike*, p. 170; Anne Perkins, *A Very British Strike 3 May–12 May 1926*, pp. 98–101, 114–16, 130; Rachelle H. Saltzman, "Folklore as Politics in Great Britain: Working-Class Critiques of Upper-Class Strike Breakers in the 1926 General Strike," *Anthropological Quarterly*, 67.3 (July 1994): 105, 107, 116, 130, https://www.jstor.org/stable/3317548.
10. Anne Perkins, *A Very British Strike 3 May–12 May 1926*, pp. 133, 135–37, 145–49; Clifford Sharp, "The Comedy of the Great English Strike," *New Republic*, 7 July 1926, https://newrepublic.com/article/90280/churchill-chamberlain-great-english-strike; Kingsley Martin, *The British Public and the General Strike* (London: Hogarth Press, 1926), pp. 23–26, 60–67, 83–85.
11. Christopher Farman, *The General Strike May 1926*, pp. 183–85; Anne Perkins, *A Very British Strike 3 May–12 May 1926*, pp. 186–91, 160–62, 166–67, 170, 172; *Beatrice Webb's Diaries 1924–1932*, pp. 97–98; Clifford Sharp, "The Comedy of the Great English Strike."
12. Anne Perkins, *A Very British Strike 3 May–12 May 1926*, pp. 173–74, 177, 179–80, 182–83; Patrick Renshaw, *The General Strike*, p. 18.
13. "The General Strike—Two Sides to Every Story!" *Hampshire Archives and Local Studies*, 23 May 2018, https://hampshirearchivesandlocalstudies.wordpress.com/2018/05/23/the-general-strike-two-sides-to-every-story/; Anne Perkins, *A Very British Strike 3 May–12 May 1926*, pp. 198–99, 202–6, 213, 244–47.
14. Keith Laybourn, *The General Strike Day by Day* (Stroud: Alan Sutton Publishing, 1996), p. 141; Keith Laybourn, *The General Strike of 1926*, p. 6; Patrick Renshaw, *The General Strike*, pp. 214, 216; Anne Perkins, *A Very British Strike 3 May–12 May 1926*, pp. 216–19, 226–32, 240; Christopher Farman, *The General Strike May 1926*, p. 239.
15. *Beatrice Webb's Diaries 1924–1932*, pp. 97–98.
16. *Beatrice Webb's Diaries 1924–1932*, pp. 124.
17. "1927 Trade Disputes Act," *Spartacus Educational*, https://spartacus-educational.com/Ltrade27.htm.

CHAPTER 6

Shaw on the British General Strike of 1926

Abstract Publicly, Shaw said almost nothing about the General Strike of 1926 while it was going on, chiefly because he was busy writing *The Intelligent Woman's Guide to Socialism and Capitalism*, published two years after the strike collapsed. In his *Guide* he says plenty, including why this strike occurred and the need for nationalization (which the country had in some services) of the coal industry to procure coal for the public at cost, *sans* profits for capitalists. Drawing on Karl Marx's famous phrase, he calls trade unionism not socialism but the capitalism of the proletariat. In a civil war between workers and capitalists, he explains that the latter try to lower wages and increase workday hours, whereas the former try to do the opposite. He points out why nationalization, while better for ordinary citizens, is less desirable than socialism. During strikes, which labor calls its only weapon, the nation suffers. In a general strike, because capitalists can hold out longer than unions can, for their reserve funds are more limited, unions invariably lose. Only a limited strike, he maintains, has promise of success.

Keywords The British General Strike of 1926 · George Bernard Shaw · *The Intelligent Woman's Guide to Socialism and Capitalism* · Nationalization · Socialism

B. F. Dukore, *Unions, Strikes, Shaw*,
Bernard Shaw and His Contemporaries,
https://doi.org/10.1007/978-3-030-99131-9_6

The British General Strike of 1926 did not change Shaw's mind that a general strike was general suicide. In the 1920s he was a global celebrity whose views newspapers frequently solicited. What may be surprising resembles what Arthur Conan Doyle, in "Silver Blaze," has Sherlock Holmes call "the curious incident of the dog in the night-time," which is that the dog did not bark, an indication that the dog was familiar with the killer. What is curious about Shaw in regard to the 1926 British General Strike is that publicly, to change the metaphor from canine to avian, he not only did not bark, he uttered barely a peep about this strike while it was on.

He gave this statement to the International News Service, dated 4 May, the first day of the strike:

> There will be nothing but coal crises until a special branch of the civil service is created to manage the coal mines as a national concern.
>
> The fact that the royal commission appointed to investigate the coal industry was afraid to say this and gave a ridiculous reason for not saying so has placed upon the Government the obligation of having a little more courage and a good deal more financial intelligence.
>
> Nationalization of private property costs the nation nothing because the purchase money is found by the proprietors, under pressure from the collectors of the income tax, the super-tax on estates, and duties.

Stressing nationalization, which he continued to do later, his statement does not mention the words "General Strike" and it appeared in only two newspapers, one the day before the strike, in Leeds, which I could not find, and one in New York, two days later (on page 1). His only other published utterance was "No time to criticize now," a cable reply to a request for an opinion on the strike, in *The World* (New York), on the strike's last day.[1] Why so little? One reason may be that Churchill commandeered paper and printing ink for the *Gazette*, leaving little for commercial newspapers and less for the *British Worker*, another is that British and American newspaper publishers were disinclined to print socialist Shaw's anti-government views of the strike, particularly since this statement offers nationalization of the coal industry as a solution to the turmoil. A third is that he was occupied writing *The Intelligent Woman's Guide to Socialism and Capitalism*. He began composing it in late 1925, complained of its difficulties during the strike, continued to work on it in 1927, and did not publish it until 1 June 1928—two years after the strike ended. He dedicated it to his sister-in-law, Mary Stewart Cholmondeley (pronounced *Chumley*), "the intelligent woman to whose question this book is the best answer I can make," who died on 5 April 1929. Shaw misspelled her name (the final *e* is omitted) in the first edition, which appears to have gone unnoticed by writers on this book, but at least one member of the family, perhaps his wife Charlotte, probably told him. His bibliography indicates the book's enormous popularity (10,000 copies had been printed in March in London and 5000 more in May prior to publication, and 75,000 in New York, of which the Book-of-the-Month Club distributed 56,000). His dedicatee's surname is spelled correctly in the book's expanded and retitled 1937 version that added Sovietism and Fascism.[2]

To eliminate high prices, which the book accurately calls overcharges, socialism proposes, by nationalizing industries, to sell goods at cost. Shaw reminds readers who fear nationalization that they already have a good deal of it, such as the postal service, the civil service, telephones, roads, and bridges. While many of their functions are also done by private companies, nationalization and municipalization are cheaper, with less costs for management and none for profits. He calls coal ripe for nationalization. Its costs are high because it is private. Scarcity raises prices, abundance lowers them. Among the ways to get scarcity are to produce less, to increase the number of those who want to buy it and can afford to pay more, and to find new uses for it. If prices fall, mines are abandoned until scarcity restores them. To keep collieries working and coal owners making large profits, prices remain high. The only owner who would work in the public's interest without a profit would be a government coalmaster-general. When coal sellers complain that nationalization means waste, high prices, the destruction of industry, and anything else they can think of at the prospect of losing profits they fail to mention the point of nationalization: "the procuring of coal for everyone at cost price."[3]

In *The Intelligent Woman's Guide*, Shaw draws on a phrase popularized by Karl Marx, "the dictatorship of the proletariat," inverting it as "Trade Unionism is not Socialism: it is the Capitalism of the Proletariat."[4] He recognized, as indicated in Chapter 3, that the unionized proletariat employed, both actually and ironically, the practice of capitalists in getting as much as possible while giving as little as possible. Whereas capitalists try to get as much labor as possible while paying workers as little as possible, unionized workers try to get as much wages and as good working conditions as possible while expending as little labor as possible. While the proletariat almost invariably lose, they lose more drastically when they expend their own financial reserves to win higher salaries and working conditions from their antagonists, since the greater financial reserves of the capitalists enable them to hold out longer than the workers can. Four years earlier, in a conversation with his biographer Archibald Henderson, Shaw used a less catchy phrase when he called trade unionism "the capitalism of the working classes." Whichever phrase one prefers, this view does not mean that Shaw turned anti-union. He was, as usual, paradoxical, not self-contradictory. As I demonstrated in Chapter 2, he believed that unions have been necessary for workers to resist submitting to salary cuts without losing their jobs. If almost all bricklayers in a town form a union, each paying small weekly dues until they have a fund to resort to when their employers try to lower wages, they can strike, live on the fund and stop the employers' business for weeks or months. They can strike against a reduction or for an increase of wages, or for fewer working hours. Employers can almost always wait until the strike fund is exhausted and the strikers starved into submission, but if business is flourishing they would lose more by closing down than by giving strikers what they want. Even so, they will bide their time until trade slackens, when they will reduce wages and lock out workers who do not accept them. Employers can always shut down without starving longer than employees can strike without enough money for food. Unless unions get concessions set by law, they would lose by lockouts what they gain by strikes. With unions, "the Proletariat and the Proprietariat face each other on a series of questions which are all parts of two main questions": will the nation hold and control land, capital, and industry or leave them with a small group of men to do with as they wish? Under capitalism, capital or labor will emerge as top dog. The alleged expense of buying out private owners, which the coal commission called an unbeatable objection to nationalizing coal mines, "is a bogey, because the coalowners (of whom, by the way, I am one) will be fully compensated, [and] the proprietary class as a whole will pay the bill out of their unearned incomes, leaving the nation richer instead of poorer by the transaction."[5]

The year before the General Strike, Shaw points out, capitalism and trade unionism exploited the state by getting a ten million pound subsidy, which the government paid the coal owners to avoid a strike, since miners refused to work unless they received certain wages and employers swore they could not afford to keep mines open unless the men accepted less. The press tried to persuade the country that excessive wages would ruin it, but the country was really prosperous. To avoid a strike that would paralyze its main industries, the government had to use tax revenues for the difference between the pay demanded and the pay offered, or to nationalize the mines. Since a capitalist government pledged not to nationalize anything, it did the former. When the ten million pounds were depleted, the problem returned. The government rejected another subsidy, the employers refused to keep mines open unless the miners worked longer hours, the miners refused to work more for less pay and workers in other industries "sympathetically" struck with them until they used up union funds for strike pay. Respectable people were frightened that the country was on the verge of revolution. During the strike the owners did not exploit taxpayers; the workers exploited them. In Shaw's view, a man on strike has no right to relief to alleviate his poverty (given as money, food, clothing or goods), but his wife and children do. Therefore, a married miner with two children received a pound a week at the expense of ratepayers while refusing to work. After the government, manned mostly by capitalists, gave miners relief (through the subsidy) at the expense of taxpayers, local authorities, mostly proletarians, gave the proletariat relief at the expense of ratepayers. In parts of London, authorities gave full relief to all who were unemployed, which freed their constituents from starvation and enabled them to hold out for higher wages. Mining districts followed suit. The capitalist government took poor laws into its own hands, recovering the weapon of starvation that proletarian local authorities took from the owners.[6]

Whereas a tenet of socialism is that idleness is indefensible, trade unionism believes in a worker's right to refuse to work (in Shaw's view, to be idle) until his demands are met. Small unions have grown and big unions have combined, thereby turning small strikes into big strikes. Electricians, railwaymen, or coal miners on strike can shut down these industries and those reliant on them, and by doing so they afflict the nation. Trade unions, now industrial unions, cover whole industries. Unions of transport and railway workers combine different trades. Their strike paralyzes the country. The government buys them off with subsidies or helps them to agree. It seeks to limit the magnitude of strikes by forbidding sympathy strikes and lockouts, but this is no remedy. Such strikes are civil wars between capital and labor while the nation suffers. Strikes are a union's "only weapon." British capitalists—who associate productive work with social inferiority, tolerate imprisonment in work-places, poverty, dirt, and drudgery—regard compulsory social service as disastrous for them and their class, which it would be.[7]

While voters may not understand socialism, says Shaw, they understand nationalization of coal mines enough to want it, at least in order to get cheaper coal. The same holds for railways and transport services. Conservatives may vote for nationalization in order to obtain cheaper traveling and lower costs for produce. A few popular nationalizations will make it as normal as old age pensions. Unions forced wage increases to miners to the point where the worst mines could not afford to operate; though opposed to socialism, the owners demanded that a conservative government give them a ten million pound subsidy in order to operate. But it was ridiculous to tax the public to keep inefficient mines in business and maintain huge prices for coal when the owners could pay decent wages, which was what the unions asked for. The subsidy stopped and a lockout followed—both avoidable had the mines been nationalized to increase wages and lower coal prices. Because proletarians inherit from unionism the idea that a strike is a weapon, they are deluded that if, instead of a coal strike here and a railway strike there, workers in all occupations struck sympathetically in a general strike to end capitalism. But in a general strike proletarians starve before the employers and capitalists, who have reserves of food. General strikes are repeatedly attempted and repeatedly fail. Those who advocate them "forget that the capitalists have never yet been so absurd as to attempt a general lockout. It would be much more sensible to support an individual strike by calling all other strikes off, thus isolating the particular employers aimed at, and enabling all the other workers to contribute to the strike fund."[8]

On 26 November 1928, two years after the end of The British General Strike of 1926 and half a year after the publication of *The Intelligent Woman's Guide*, Shaw gave a speech in support of the Miners' Distress Fund in which his humor seemed to belie his heartfelt views:

> I cannot speak of the condition of the miners, because I have not been to the coalfields and do not know. My early experience of poverty made me firmly resolved never to get into contact with it again. I have never been down a coalmine because no one has ever offered to pay me to do so, and I can imagine no human being wanting to go down one unless he was very handsomely paid.

Nor, he continued, could he "pretend to be a disinterested friend of the poor." If no one were to do anything for them, "then the Government would have to do something, and would have to get money out of the pockets of the supertax payers." Since he himself was one of these payers, he found himself "in the deplorable position of asking you to put your hands in your pockets to prevent the Government putting its hand in mine." After laughter greeted this, he continued to leaven his earnestness with his familiar wit:

> A nation which allows its men to go underground to live without ultra-violet rays is in a condition bordering on lunacy. I hope the day will come when all the coalmines are shut up—I will not say with the proprietors inside. There is plenty of power above ground waiting to be intelligently tackled. In the north of Scotland, by using turbines to harness the tide you could get enough power to run all Europe. There would be plenty of work for the unemployed. Why don't we do it? Because we are a people bordering on lunacy. I am always telling English people that, but somehow they seem to like it.

After the laughter died down, his seriousness became more evident: "I hope sooner or later we shall see that there is plenty of employment if only we arrange things properly, instead of letting one man do fourteen hours' work a day while there is another man idle only too anxious to do half for him."[9]

Notes

1. G. Bernard Shaw, "Shaw Sees Crisis Upon Crisis Until Government Takes Control of Mines," *New York American*, 5 May 1926, p. 1; "No Time to Criticise Now," Dan H. Laurence, *Bernard Shaw: A Bibliography* (Oxford: Clarendon Press, 1983), Vol. 2, p. 708 (C2595, C2596).
2. Bernard Shaw, *The Intelligent Woman's Guide to Socialism and Capitalism* (London: Constable, 1928), p. v; Bernard Shaw, *The Intelligent Woman's Guide to Socialism, Capitalism, Sovietism and Fascism* (London: Constable, 1949), p. v; Dan H. Laurence, *Bernard Shaw: A Bibliography* (Oxford: Clarendon Press, 1983), Vol. 1, pp. 172–73.
3. Bernard Shaw, *The Intelligent Woman's Guide to Socialism, Capitalism, Sovietism and Fascism*, pp. 105–10.
4. Marx's full phrase (in translation) is "the class struggle necessarily leads to the dictatorship of the proletariat," which he wrote in a letter to Joseph Weydemeyer, 5 March 1852; Archibald Henderson, *Table-Talk of G.B.S.*

(New York: Harper & Brothers, 1925), p. 154. According to the *Oxford Dictionary of Quotations*, Third Edition (1986), Marx's phrase had been used two years earlier in the constitution of the World Society of Revolutionary Communists, signed by Marx, Engels and others. The phrase was probably common among German socialists at the time, including Weydemeyer, who had used it, before Marx's letter, as the title of his article "The Dictatorship of the Proletariat," first published in *Turn-Zeitung* (New York), 1 January 1852: "The Dictatorship of the Proletariat—Joseph Weydemeyer," *libcom* (Library of Communism), https://libcom.org/library/dictatorship-proletariat-joseph-weydemeyer.

5. Bernard Shaw, *The Intelligent Woman's Guide to Socialism, Capitalism, Sovietism and Fascism*, pp. 186, 204–6, 213, 223, 274.
6. Bernard Shaw, *The Intelligent Woman's Guide to Socialism, Capitalism, Sovietism and Fascism*, pp. 301–3.
7. Bernard Shaw, *The Intelligent Woman's Guide to Socialism, Capitalism, Sovietism and Fascism*, pp. 355–58.
8. Bernard Shaw, *The Intelligent Woman's Guide to Socialism, Capitalism, Sovietism and Fascism*, pp. 383, 387–88, 448–49.
9. "Mr. Shaw as the 'Star' Turns: Miners' Fund Appeal," *Manchester Guardian*, 26 November 1928, p. 10.

CHAPTER 7

Socialism, Nationalization, and *Major Barbara*

Abstract Shaw contrasts socialism and nationalization. He sees Fabian methods as surer of success than workers rushing to the barricades. *Major Barbara* demonstrates that improvements in the living conditions of laborers, which are possible under capitalism, are desirable even without socialism. As Kingsley Martin discerns, Shaw's dialectical methods make his plays debates in which no one wins but everyone scores.

Keywords Socialism · Nationalization · Fabianism · *Major Barbara*

Arguing against Shaw's view of unionism, nationalization, and socialism, Gareth Griffith disparages Shaw's "hostility" toward and "distrust" of the Labour Party. He scoffs at a statement Shaw made in 1907: "Only the Fabian Party, he announced in all seriousness, [is] headed straight for socialism."[1] By contrast, I find this remark refreshing after Shaw's familiar defensiveness, as in 1890: "If, in Hamlet's phrase, we are 'pigeon livered, and lack gall to make oppression bitter,' Fabian will come to mean nothing but an excuse for not fighting. I am afraid some of our recently acquired middle class vogue is due to the impression that we have found out a way of making socialism itself an excuse for exhorting the working class not to do anything rash." He wanted Parliament to enact laws giving

B. F. Dukore, *Unions, Strikes, Shaw*,
Bernard Shaw and His Contemporaries,
https://doi.org/10.1007/978-3-030-99131-9_7

the working class control of the "coercive force of police and soldiery which are the sole bulwark of Private Property today." Such measures will pass only when Parliament becomes convinced that if they do not, the workers will use force. Shaw does not mean that workers should rush to the barricades, as in novels.[2] Fabian methods and barricades methods, he said in 1904, are not unconnected. "The mistake... is not in believing that the revolution will be effected by force, but in putting the fighting at the wrong end of the process." Years of parliamentary activity are needed in order to prepare the English to storm the barricades.[3]

Unlike Griffith's, the usual take on Shaw is that of Alick West, who titled his book "*A Good Man Fallen Among Fabians*."[4] He emphasizes *fallen*, but the quotation, by Lenin, emphasizes *good*. Lenin also called Shaw "a great deal further left than his company."[5] Griffith points out that Lenin derided Shaw's *Fabianism and the Empire* as indicative of Fabian's "social chauvinism" and, astutely, that the degree to which Lenin changed world politics "seems beyond the scope of the Fabian imagination." Because "the opportunity to exercise authority is limited by class," Griffith writes, conservatives conclude that farming and industrial laborers are unfit to cope with social responsibility. Shaw might have supported "participatory democracy in industry," but he did not. Griffith singles out *Major Barbara* as stressing "strict hierarchy in working relations," with Undershaft saying that whereas his workers theoretically rebel against him, in practice each one "keeps the man just below him in his place." He omits Shaw's emphasis, a few sentences later, that Undershaft boasts he is thoroughly capitalist: "The result is a colossal profit, which comes to me." Shaw does not give Undershaft the final word or unequivocal victory. Griffith also pinpoints "a hierarchical twist" in "the militant speeches of Cusins, the heir apparent," quoting, "As a teacher of Greek I gave the intellectual man an intellectual weapon against the poor man. I now want to give the common man weapons against the intellectual man," and "I want to arm them against" the professional people "who, once in authority, are more disastrous and tyrannical" than the fools and scoundrels. He would prefer Cusins to "seek a power which might allow the common man to use his own genius for his own good."[6] I submit that Cusins's lines are character-driven, from his background as a teacher of Greek. While Griffith admits the play is not "conclusive evidence of Shaw's views" since it is characters who speak, rather than the author, he mocks, "Every bone in [Shaw's] Fabian body warned him of the dangers of unregulated working-class activism; every imperative of his morality of service condemned strikes as a form of anti-social activity, with the right to strike being viewed as the worker's right to idleness." In my view, Kingsley Martin has a more appropriate assessment of Shaw, whose "debates became plays" in which "no one won, though everyone scored."[7]

Shaw knew that nationalization differed from socialism and he recognized, as John Jewkes puts it, that nationalization was "a piecemeal and empirical approach to much wider ideas."[8] To Shaw, raising the standard of living for workers and nationalizing industries were stepping-stones to socialism. The year before he wrote *Major Barbara*, London papers contained reports that the Krupp firm in Essen, Germany, had built the largest housing colonies in Europe, with 4300 separate dwelling places for Krupp workers. In them, at Krupp's expense, were playgrounds, a church, and nondenominational elementary schools for children of the firm's employees. The Krupp welfare plan provided for sickness relief, hospitals, homes for the aged, pensions, widows' and orphans' funds, and life insurance. Like Undershaft's firm in *Major Barbara*, as I quoted in the last paragraph, Sidney P. Albert reports that at the same time the Krupp armaments business "profited from them as much as the workers benefited." Undershaft's factory is an intermediary that provides higher wages and better living conditions for workers than other factory owners usually do. If capitalists are willing to create these benefits before nationalization or socialism comes about, it would be ill-advised not to praise these stages of advancement. Nationalization is a reasonable and doable form of progress. "If the owners will not pay subsistence wages," Shaw warned, "the nation must; for it cannot afford to have its children under-nourished... though it was fool enough to think it could in Queen Victoria's time. Subsidies and doles are demoralizing, both for employers and proletarians; but they stave off Socialism, which people seem to consider worse than pauperized insolvency."[9] If the nation must do so, then why should one object to capitalists who do so before this? And as he was aware, staving off differs from substituting for. An essential part of Shaw's view is compensation to owners of nationalized assets. What is often overlooked or derided by adverse critics of this position, as he dramatizes in *On the Rocks*, which the next chapter analyzes, is that, as Mary Bell Cairns states, "the principle of compensation for assets compulsorily transferred from private to public ownership has long been established in English law," dating from at least the sixteenth century. When, after World War II, Parliament nationalized numerous industries, all of the Acts contained "a provision relative to the payment of taxes or other charges: 'Nothing in this Act shall be deemed to exempt the Commission from liability for any tax, duty, rate, levy or other charge whatsoever, whether general or local.'"[10]

Notes

1. Gareth Griffith, *Socialism and Superior Brains* (London: Routledge, 1995), pp. 85–86.
2. Reprinted in Bernard Shaw, "Socialism and Human Nature," *The Road to Equality*, ed. Louis Crompton and Hilayne Cavanagh (Boston: Beacon Press, 1971), pp. 101–2.
3. This quotation, which is uncited, is in Eric Bentley, *Bernard Shaw 1856–1950* (New York: New Directions, 1957), pp. 11–12.
4. Alick West, *A Good Man Fallen Among Fabians* (London: Lawrence & Wishart, 1950).
5. The Lenin quotation is from Vladimir Scherbina, *Lenin and the Problems of Literature* (Moscow: Progress Publishers, 1974), pp. 90–91; see also pp. 68, 239; Bernard F. Dukore, *Money & Politics in Ibsen, Shaw and Brecht* (Columbia: University of Missouri Press, 1980), pp. xvii–xix.
6. Gareth Griffith, *Socialism and Superior Brains*, pp. 68, 89–90, 239; the *Major Barbara* quotations are from Bernard Shaw, *Collected Plays with Their Prefaces*, ed. Dan H. Laurence (London: Max Reinhardt, 1971), Vol. 3, pp. 154–55, 181.
7. Gareth Griffith, *Socialism and Superior Brains*, p. 89; Kingsley Martin, "G.B.S." *Shaw and Society*, ed. C.E.M. Joad (London: Odhams Press, 1953), p. 31.
8. John Jewkes, "The Nationalization of Industry," *University of Chicago Law Review*, 20.4 (Summer 1953): 615, https://core.ac.uk/download/pdf/234131715.pdf.
9. Sidney P. Albert, "Evangelizing the Garden City?" *SHAW: The Annual of Bernard Shaw Studies: Shaw and History*, ed. Gale K. Larson (1999), 19: 49–50. The Shaw quotation, not cited, is in St. John Ervine, Bernard Shaw: *His Life, Work and Friends* (New York: William Morrow, 1956), p. 514.
10. Mary Bell Cairns, "Some Legal Aspects of Compensation for Nationalized Assets," *Law and Contemporary Problems*, 16 (Fall 1951): 594–95, https://core.ac.uk/download/pdf/194445211.pdf; M.L.S., "British Nationalization of Industry—Compensation to Owners of Expropriated Property," *University of Pennsylvania Law Review*, 97 (1949): 520, 540, https://scholarship.law.upenn.edu/cgi/viewcontent.cgi?article=8769&context=penn_law_review.

CHAPTER 8

On the Rocks and Nationalization

Abstract Shaw wrote one play whose themes include the subjects of this book, *On the Rocks*, which was first performed during the Great Depression. Unable to cope with the depression's results—millions unemployed—the British prime minister comes to recognize that the Government's initial solutions should be to nationalize ground rent and leases, municipalize urban land, and eliminate land taxes and tariffs, replacing them by foreign trade in state-protected industries, whose products the state would sell at regulated prices, with profits, if any, accruing to the country. The government would replace individual farming with collective farming, double the surtax on income derived from investments, abolish inheritance taxes, and mandate compulsory service for everyone, as in wartime. With the nation controlling industry, it would confiscate property and give compensation to its owners. As expected, cabinet members, who are or are allied with capitalists oppose these. So do unions, which resist his goal to outlaw strikes.

Keywords Socialism · Nationalization · Fabianism · George Bernard Shaw · *On the Rocks*

B. F. Dukore, *Unions, Strikes, Shaw*,
Bernard Shaw and His Contemporaries,
https://doi.org/10.1007/978-3-030-99131-9_8

Not until the Great Depression did Shaw write a play containing major themes that are the subjects of this book, *On the Rocks* (1933), whose two acts may be considered Before and After. What happens between them is akin to a Pauline revelation on the road to Damascus. Prime Minister Sir Arthur Chavender's eye-opener, which is a political not a religious epiphany, occurs in Wales, where a doctor treats his malady, which she diagnoses as a "common English complaint, an underworked brain." Her therapy is denying him newspapers and letters, and permitting him to read books only in the afternoon, after he has spent the morning thinking. His revelation comes from reading Marx, Lenin, Trotsky, and Stalin—who, the play fails to mention, had expelled Trotsky from the Soviet Union four years earlier (in 1940 Stalin would succeed in having Trotsky murdered).[1]

Before leaving London for Wales he made feeble excuses for his inaction on unemployment and methods of reviving the economy: "Do you suppose I would not revive trade... tomorrow if I could?" he pleads. But he calls himself "in the grip of economic forces that are beyond human control. What mortal man could do this Government has done." This does not prevent him from boasting that he has "saved the people from starvation by stretching unemployment benefit to the utmost limit of our national resources," at which claim a Labour delegate interrupts him to point out that he cut unemployment compensation to fifteen shillings and shoved every beneficiary he could off it with a means test. When he maintains that "there is still an immense fringe of the human race growing up to a sense of the necessity for British goods," the seasoned Labourite Old Hipney sets him straight on what we now, but not he then, call outsourcing: "All goods is alike to that lot provided theyre the cheapest.... A Chinese coolie can live on a penny a day. What can we do against labor at a penny a day...?" When all Chavender can muster up is cant that "Our workers must make sacrifices," Hipney reminds him that it is he whom they will sacrifice. All that English workers want is jobs, so that they could feed themselves and their families, and be "comfortable according to their notion of comfort." If he had enabled them to do that, he would not have the problems he has; but he has not been equal to the challenge. No one on earth, he avows, is "more helpless than what our factories and machines have made of an English working man when nobody will give him a job and pay him to do it."[2]

Upon returning to London from Wales, Chavender straightaway initiates a program of reforms, key pieces of which are the nationalization of ground rent and ground leases (fees for land with buildings), which had been common in Britain since feudal times for banks, collieries, transport, and fertilizers, along with the municipalization of urban land and the elimination of land taxes. Instead of tariffs, he would prohibit foreign trade in government-protected industries and legalize imports by the state, and he would sell the import at regulated prices. Collective farming would renovate agriculture. He would double the surtax on unearned income (primarily returns on investments), abolish inheritance taxes (which are another form of unearned income) and mandate compulsory service for everyone, as the government had done during the Great War. He would restore wage cuts in the military and police, increase their forces by five thousand people whose salaries he would raise by 10 percent, and would add aircraft-carrying battleships to the navy. Although he does not offer something for everyone, he offers enough for so many that he and his supporters believe his program will pass.[3]

Chavender does not anticipate opposition from the Labour Party or unions. When a labor delegation from the Isle of Cats—an alias for the Isle of Dogs, an area (not an island) in the East End—arrives (the same delegation that had visited him in the first act), he greets them as "the voice of the proletariat." To his astonishment, the mayor, "*rudely*" objecting to extreme left-wing lingo, responds, "Who are you calling the proletariat? Do you take us for Communists?" How can Chavender imagine that the mayor's constituents would vote for compulsory labor and the elimination of the right to strike, which they consider their only weapon against capitalists. Using Chavender as his raisonneur in this scene, Shaw has the prime minister explain that strikes amount to what he, in his own person, had called the right to starve and adversely influence public opinion, as I have quoted earlier. "Which of you starves first when it comes to the point?" Chavender asks rhetorically. The mayor rebukes him. If he thinks British workers will approve compulsory labor and eliminating strikes, he knows nothing of the real world—which Shaw recognizes is the case. But compulsory labor would not affect those with jobs, Chavender tries to clarify, only idlers. To the unionists this is claptrap, the real meaning of which is, as one Labourite states, "Keep all the soft jobs for your lot and the hard ones for us." A plutocrat who is present tries to explain the importance of nationalizing land; he is rebuffed because of the issue of compensation: "Take the land with one hand and give back its cash value to the landlords with the other!" A duke explains that because he and his like will pay for compensation through income tax, surtax, and estate tax, the workers will get the money back. The suspicious unionists steadfastly refuse their support. The duke laments, "Chained dogs are the fiercest guardians of property; and those who attempt to unchain them are the first to be bitten."[4]

One weakness of Shaw's position is his failure to respond convincingly to the view that a strike is a union's only weapon, or that he would retain strikes for local use, as I have described earlier. Another is his understanding of "the idle." By calling workers idle because they are not in factories, on railroad trains, or at desks, but are in picket lines, is to misuse the term, which equates these people with the "idle rich," whose income is not from their labor. To some extent, Shaw's notion of a union comes from his own union, which represents writers, not blue-collar physical laborers or white-collar office workers. In 1920 he predicted, with wild inaccuracy, "The Trade union as we knew it would pass away by transformation into a Professional Association." Perhaps there is something to the "uncomfortable intuition" of his sister, Lucy Carr Shaw, who on 26 June 1901 used this phrase in a letter to a friend, about her perception of her brother's change of fortune: "The luxurious life he leads now is so much the reverse of the old ascetic one, that it must influence his mental vision".[5]

In *On the Rocks* Old Hipney, who is disillusioned with democracy, complains that Parliament will "never do anything" and calls Guy Fawkes the only person who understood Parliament (he tried to blow it up). He objects, biblically, that expanded suffrage "delivered us into the hands of our spoilers" (Judges 2:14). Chavender urges him not to throw out the baby with the bathwater. If people have no voice in the government, and no choice of who will represent them, it will be bad for them.[6] Both Hipney and Chavender speak for Shaw, whose plays are dialectical. In his lecture "In Praise of Guy Fawkes," delivered the year before he wrote *On the Rocks*, Shaw complained, like Hipney, that Parliament prevents the Government from governing. Like Chavender, Shaw promoted "the municipalization and nationalization of land, the national control of industry, the accumulation of capital by the State, the regulation of foreign trade." It should be no surprise—see the quotation about professional associations in the previous paragraph—that Shaw's views were not always on the mark. His Guy Fawkes speech refers to a recent election: "The whole of America was swept in one headlong rush to substitute Mr Roosevelt for Mr Hoover. The substitution will not make the slightest difference to any American."[7] Wrong. While Shaw was writing the play Roosevelt stopped people from withdrawing money from banks, got Congress to pass an Act to reorganize them and close insolvent ones, signed Acts that built dams on the Tennessee River, paid farmers to let their fields lie fallow to end surpluses (and also to let the land regenerate, thereby increasing the soil's productivity) and made loans to homeowners; he soon guaranteed rights to unionize and established a public works program.

Notes

1. Bernard Shaw, *On the Rocks*, *Collected Plays with Their Prefaces*, ed. Dan H. Laurence (London: Max Reinhardt, 1973), Vol. 6, pp. 667, 671–72, 676.
2. Bernard Shaw, *On the Rocks*, Vol. 6, pp. 653–59.
3. Bernard Shaw, *On the Rocks*, Vol. 6, pp. 680–83.
4. Bernard Shaw, *On the Rocks*, Vol. 6, pp. 692–95, 701.
5. Allan Chappelow, *Shaw—"The Chucker-Out"* (London: George Allen and Unwin, 1969), p. 294; the letter is in Henry George Farmer, *Bernard Shaw's Sister and Her Friends* (Leiden: E.J. Brill, 1959), p. 138.
6. Bernard Shaw, *On the Rocks*, Vol. 6, pp. 717, 719–20.
7. Bernard Shaw, "In Praise of Guy Fawkes," *Platform and Pulpit*, ed. Dan H. Laurence (New York: Hill and Wang, 1961), pp. 239–40.

CHAPTER 9

Conclusion

Abstract Shaw's solutions, raising questions of whether or in what instances he was fallible and in what circumstances he may have been right, treats his lifetime and afterward, encapsulating political and administrative criteria about their validity in social and economic terms. It deals with strikes and privatization in the U.K. and the U.S. as well as union-breaking actions by Thatcher, Reagan, and Trump, relating them to union-management conflicts when Shaw was alive and active, and to statements and actions in previous chapters.

Keywords Socialism · Nationalization · Private ownership · Strikes · Unions · George Bernard Shaw

Like everyone, Shaw is fallible. Might unions devise something more effective than massive strikes? Must they be the capitalism of the proletariat? Is it not possible that his immediate or at least interim solution, nationalization, may have been a good idea? As he admits, unions were necessary to enable workers to obtain higher pay, improved hours of employment, and better working conditions. True, general strikes mostly fail, since with more money to fall back on, owners are able to hold out longer than strikers are; when the government intervenes, it usually favors

B. F. Dukore, *Unions, Strikes, Shaw*,
Bernard Shaw and His Contemporaries,
https://doi.org/10.1007/978-3-030-99131-9_9

the owners; and when the owners submit to union demands, they wait until the time is ripe for reversion to the *status quo ante*. Yet Britain's nationalization during World War I succeeded. No data proves that it was more inept than private ownership, as the mine owners charged. In Shaw's England and in America, then and now, most workers do not consider themselves communists or socialists. We know today that countries calling themselves communist or socialist are such in name only. In the United States, Franklin D. Roosevelt's New Deal succeeded insofar as his conservative opponents could not stop it, but after they regained power much later, they cut, changed, or refused to provide funding that would enforce much of it.

In the early twentieth century, John Jewkes indicates, "socialist writers claimed broad social advantages of nationalization." In 1946 Labour Party Prime Minister Clement Attlee's government passed legislation that included the Coal Industry Nationalisation Act, establishing the National Coal Board, which received responsibility for managing and running the coal industry. Then, and more recently, proponents of privatized ownership raised questions of whether nationalization replaced inefficient systems with more inefficient systems and whether it raised or lowered the standard of living. To Jewkes, who analyzed the concept of nationalization in Britain eight years after it was instituted, measuring changes in efficiency by reference to "figures of physical output in terms of physical input, so-called yardsticks, is a chimera." If the standards of price, cost, and profit are discarded or are "inapplicable, no other statistics have any great significance." He found it impossible to give simple estimates for net gains from large-scale operations of nationalized industries so soon. Suggestions to measure the many institutional changes that might improve "the 'accountability' of nationalized industries are largely beating the air, for increased intelligence or energy on the part of those who are to employ the yardstick is of no account till the yardstick exists." Students of industrial organization cannot render final judgments on whether or not nationalization is good since judgments are based on established or proposed standards of worthiness. However, they can, and he did, examine the major changes accomplished by nationalization, such as monopolistic control and non-profit seeking actions, question the claims made for them and assess, as much as data permit, how valid these claims are. It is impossible to provide a simple estimate for gains that arise from large-scale operations of nationalized industries. "Perhaps the safest and the fairest deduction is that, in presenting the case for and against nationalization, specific economies of scale could hardly be a crucial item one way or another." It is striking that in public discussions of nationalized industries, their size is not an accepted virtue but has become persistently problematic. "The great debate has not been about the achievements made possible by the increased scale of operation but how best the public boards can overcome the defects and difficulties associated with their size, of how best they can circumvent just the kind of troubles long familiar to large organizations." The emphasis on decentralization in nationalized industries is evidence that size has come to be considered a liability, not an asset. While mine workers and unions favored and favor nationalization—which, Tejvan Pettinger, in 2019, calls understandable, since "they feel they may be better treated by the government rather than a profit maximising monopoly"—mine owners or former owners insisted and insist, perhaps with a touch of hypocrisy, that its increased size makes administration more difficult, even though, as Jewkes pointed out earlier, they make no similar claim for such larger private corporations as General Motors, Imperial Chemical Industries, and Du Pont, which continue to generate huge profits.[1]

In April 2021 Nathan Osafao Omane, a U.K. corporate officer and accountant, favors private ownership over nationalization of coal mines, which Britain's Coal Industry Act of 1994 privatized. Although he recognizes the emergence of cheaper energy sources, the increased availability of oil in the North Sea and elsewhere, and nuclear power, he calls them unimportant because "*If* coal had remained under private control" the diseconomies of the coal industry "*might have* remained competitive for much longer" (my italics)—which is argument by conjecture, not data, and is therefore of questionable value. He also argues that the National Coal Board failed because its initial early members and chairman were not chosen for "their managerial acumen. Three of the Board's eight chairmen had no executive experience prior to managing the Board" and the first chairman, Alfred Robens, "had no experience in the energy industry." Although these points are valid, they apply to particular individuals, not to nationalization as such.[2]

The same year, an article in the *International Mining Congress*, by D.W. Dixon-Hardy and I.G. Ediz, was skeptical about the U.K.'s privatized coal industry, which took effect on 1 January 1995. In order to ease the transition from public to private ownership, the British Coal Corporation allowed independent operators, for a short time, "to take over coal mines under 'lease and licence' arrangements." Most of them sold coal at a price set before privatization. Investing up to a billion pounds in newly discovered coal reserves that promised hundreds of tonnes (which weigh more than tons) of coal and numerous jobs, private corporations acquired hundreds of square kilometers of land in England, with promises of more to come. Initially, they had "a relatively 'easy' time." In the late 1990s, however, because of the collapse of world coal prices, this plan failed to proceed. As these authors state, "The main or perhaps the ultimate purpose of a business is to produce a profit for its shareholders," and benefits to the community are a hope. Unless companies "have an ethical policy in place to deal with U.K.-based suppliers, even at a possible reduction in profit," owners of other businesses have "no moral obligation... to support the U.K. coal industry." Considering the nation's history of relations among coal mine owners, workers, unions, and the public, "bad feelings" caused by market difficulties are almost inevitable. The ability of mining companies to stay in business depends on the prices they can command for their coal, which numerous factors determine. As in the United States, there were movements toward gas as a preferred fuel to generate power (called in the U.K. "the Dash for Gas") and concerns about the environment. The need to reduce the emission of greenhouse gases was among the contributing factors to the problems of the coal industry. Inevitably, politics and political propaganda played major roles in the privatized coal industries of both countries. In the U.K. the Labour Party reminds the press that a previous conservative government privatized the coal industry, as well as power stations, the grid system, and the electricity-purchasing system, whereas in America the Republican Party tries to frighten the electorate that energy sources other than coal and gasoline are job-destroyers, more expensive, inefficient and unreliable. Apropos the U.K., Dixon-Hardy and Ediz observe what might be considered heretical in the United States: "The privatised coal industry today may well have been radically different if controlling interests in power generation were controlled by mining-friendly organisations" or when the times became "more environmentally friendly." After this book's account of British coal mining strikes and the issue of government subsidies in the first half of the last century, readers may have a sense of *déjà vu* at their report that "Coal mining companies considered that the government's ban on new gas stations was a step in the right direction, but that it might prove to be too little too late and argued that subsidies should be offered to mining industries to avoid pit closures," and that the government intends for "recent subsidies allocated to coal operators... to be short-term in nature," because long-term subsidies are not politically viable. "Concerns over world oil prices, how many years of North Sea gas reserves will be available, the true cost of nuclear power and the contribution to power generation from renewable sources are all factors in whether coal will continue to be mined in the U.K."[3]

According to Jewkes, the only potent criticism of nationalized industries is that, after having been taken out of pre-nationalization politics in Great Britain they are subjected to different political pressures or ideologies, of which the appointment of the chairman mentioned above, a member of the governing Labour Party, may be an example. Political pressures on unions are true in the United States as well. In 1935 Franklin D. Roosevelt signed the National Labor Relations Act, which recognized the right of employees to organize in order to collectively bargain for fair contracts. Although business groups supported management's right to make job and political rules, the Supreme Court upheld this Act in 1937. Businesses of all sizes tried to undermine the decision, and in 1944 they contrived a solution in holding so-called right-to-work referendums in Florida, Arkansas, and California. Because union contracts cover nonunion as well as union members, union rules ensure that everyone benefits from the union gains, including the former, who get a free ride on the contributions of the latter, which as Chapter 1 describes, Shaw disparaged as dishonorable freeloading or leeching. Local and national opponents of the Act, including the National Association of Manufacturers, the U.S. Chamber of Commerce, the National Labor-Management Foundation, and the Christian American Association shrewdly used ballot initiatives to pass right-to-work propositions, vastly outspending unions on newspaper, radio, and television advertisements with claims that these propositions would free workers from union bosses determined to deny their freedom to choose whether or not to join a union. As a *Washington Post* columnist phrased it recently, "So-called right-to-work laws have always been sold as all-American protections of individual freedoms," but they confuse restrictions on Americans' basic rights on the job. "These statutes empower employers by undermining workers' right to organize and rolling back the gains—better wages, working conditions and hours—that unions fought to secure."[4]

Among the conspicuous English anti-unionists is Margaret Thatcher, who—determined not to have her career as prime minister destroyed like that of her predecessor (Edward Heath, also a conservative)—crushed the

National Union of Mineworkers (NUM) in 1985, the year after its strike began. Although those on the left and those on the right agree that she broke trade unionism in the U.K., they describe it differently. The former say that she destroyed unions and ruined the nation's economy; the latter, that she tamed unions and restored the economy. Both probably agree, as one observer states, that she and United States President Ronald Reagan "were cheerleaders for the economics of free-trade, state-shrinking and deregulation," but disagree that these "helped to bring about the decline of manufacturing employment in most western countries." Along with these changes, union membership fell in both countries. Like the General Strike of 1926, the NUM strike in 1984–1985 gained sympathy from other unions and from the public; and both strikes ended in failure. In the 1970s decade, strikes had closed every British coal mine, and a combination of solidarity strikes by other unions and targeted picketing stopped the country's industry, which as just indicated led to the downfall of Heath. Shrewdly, Thatcher analyzed how the miners had done this and understood how to avoid the same fate. After she attained power in 1979, B.P. Perry writes, "she had her ministers and civil servants draw up secret plans that would keep coal moving around the country were the miners to attempt another strike." By the 1980s, coal production became more unprofitable and, as in the 1920s, the industry banked on government subsidies. Thatcher, who had streamlined the country's steel industry by eliminating 95,000 jobs and closing plants, which resulted in a change from an annual loss of £1.6 billion to almost a profit, became enabled to privatize that industry, which she also wanted to do with coal. Unlike 1926, however, the 1984 coal miners' union leader had not asked for a national ballot before calling a strike. Thus, coal miners did not unanimously or near-unanimously go on strike. Furthermore, says Perry, "Thatcher had secretly stockpiled supplies of both coal and coke in strategic sites around the country; her government had also entered into agreements with non-unionised haulage firms to break the pickets and carry the coal from storage facilities and coking plants to power stations and factories." Unlike 1972 and 1974, the nation experienced no power cuts and like 1926 the government was not forced to negotiate. Also as in 1926, Thatcher controlled a formidable weapon, the police. "In the 1970s, the police had treated the miners with kid gloves," whereas in the 1980s the gloves came off. As in Pennsylvania in 1877 and New Zealand in 1913, both related in Chapter 4, police from outside an affected city and county were brought in "to prevent picketing and strike action, and to ensure no disruption to supply lines." This begat violent clashes between the picketers and the police, who launched mounted truncheon charges against the miners. The stalemate produced by Thatcher's preparations lasted a year. Life for miners and their families became more difficult. A changed law deprived the dependents of miners of benefits, and as union funds ran dry, destitute miners trickled back to work through picket lines. "Organisationally," Nicholas Jones states, "the killer blow for the unions was the end of the closed shop and withdrawal of 'check-off' agreements that required employers to deduct union contributions."[5]

Nationalization was not at stake in the candidacy or political career of Ronald Reagan, a former union president (of the Screen Actors' Guild from 1947 to 1952 and from 1959 to 1960) who became another union breaker. In 1981, a year and a half after his first inauguration as president, he destroyed the Professional Air Traffic Controllers Organization (PATCO), which had been one of the few unions that endorsed him during his election campaign, when the union went on strike. During his campaign he had written to PATCO's director, expressing sympathy with "the deplorable state of our nation's air traffic control system," in which "too few people [were] working unreasonable hours with obsolete equipment," and pledged to "work very closely" with the union to remedy this. In 1981, however, he reversed his pledge: "They are in violation of the law, and if they do not report for work within 48 hours, they have forfeited their jobs and will be terminated." They did not report for work. Using provisions of the Taft-Hartley Act, he made good on his threat, replacing them—a tactic that recalls William Martin Murphy's for Irish strikers earlier in the century, noted in Chapter 4—with the Federal Aviation Administration's supervisors, non-striking controllers, and military controllers, who filled in for the picketers. As a team of the legal writers and editors of *FindLaw* state, The Taft-Hartley Act, just mentioned, "expressly authorizes the states to pass laws prohibiting union shops," also called closed shops, which required all employees to pay union dues whether or not they were formal members of the union and whether or not they agreed with its contributions to political campaigns. Based on this Act, many states (currently twenty-eight) enacted limitations on unions, commonly called "right to work laws." In these states workers need not join or pay dues to unions that represent them.[6]

What Reagan and members of his administration may not have known is that Great Britain was beforehand on this issue. In 1909 the Osborne Judgement, to which I alluded in Chapter 1, based on a case brought by a Liberal Party supporter who objected that his union used his dues for a political purpose to which "he was hostile" (contributions to what he considered a socialist party). The House of Lords found for him in ruling that the law did not allow trade unions to collect a levy for political purposes, specifically, to fund the Labour Party's "organisational and electoral efforts." The 1913 Trade Union Act modified this decision, giving unions "the right to divide its subscriptions into a political and a social fund." If union members like Osborne objected to political contributions, they could opt out of this part of their dues. The year after the 1926 General Strike, the conservative government passed the Trade Disputes and Trade Unions Act, alluded to in Chapter 5, which deliberately damaged the Labour Party "by forcing union members to make a positive decision to pay a levy to a political party." Instead of opting out, union members had to "contract in," which was more difficult and which resulted in the Labour Party losing about a third of its income. In 1940, Ronald Sires states, the TUC "'unanimously passed a resolution' asking its representatives in the coalition cabinet to gain concessions" from Prime Minister Winston Churchill. In 1941 Churchill insisted that every effort should be on winning the war, putting questions of repeal or amendments on hold until victory. After World War II, Labour Prime Minister Clement Attlee called the Act of 1927 "'an act of injustice in the minds of trade unionists'" that "'deprived great bodies of citizens of the rights of free association which they had enjoyed' for many years without abuse'" and called for its removal. In 1946 Parliament repealed this 1927 Act.[7]

As with Reagan, nationalization of industries was not an issue in the campaign or administration of Donald Trump, whose entire career, before and after his election as president, was marked by anti-unionism. Ironically, he received more votes from union households than his two Republican predecessors had got in their failed election bids. As president, he made it easier to fire union and nonunion federal workers, limited the amount of work time that union officers and stewards could utilize for union activities and made it easier for employers to restrict employee rights to talk to their co-workers about a union during working hours, even to ask a coworker to join one. He also appointed corporate executives and anti-union lawyers to lead agencies in charge of protecting workers' rights: the Department of Labor and the National Labor Relations Board. Recalling Churchill's charge of "cosmopolitan conspirators" in the General Strike of 1926, quoted in Chapter 5, Trump and his supporters railed and continue to rail against metropolitan "elites." One of them, U.S. Senator Josh Hawley of Missouri, in a 2019 speech at the National Conservatism Conference, used Churchill's term, no doubt unknowingly, when he chastised global corporations for "investing their profits not in American workers, not in American development, but in financial instruments that benefit the cosmopolitan elite," leaving middle America with "flat wages, with lost jobs, with declining investment and declining opportunity."[8]

When we remember the hopes and emotions that nationalization stimulated, says Jewkes, it may be that its early believers "were on much firmer ground in appealing to its social virtues," for if a community believes that "profit making and the private ownership of industrial capital are so repugnant to its ethical standards that it must replace them," then economists have nothing to say. However, if one assumes that "the search for what is considered morally right will also lead to a pot of gold, that doing good will also bring an economic bonus, then it would seem that this is just another rainbow in the sky."[9]

What of the income gap in the nineteenth and early twentieth centuries, compared to today's, that is, between the Gilded Age and Gilded Age 2.0, cited in Chapter 1? And what of social safety nets in the present-day United States and the liberal welfare state of today's U.K.? Of course these make a difference that would be folly to minimize. Yet the gap persists. It did not begin with the Covid-19 pandemic, which exacerbated it and made more people aware of it than would have been the case if it had not inflicted the world.

Notwithstanding the wealth generated by the industrial revolution, private ownership of land was the chief basis of wealth in Victorian England. Starting about 1870, Peter Lindert observed over thirty years ago, "Critics attacked the landed class for being wealthy and for exacting an unearned increment from their tenants, especially their Irish tenants." Although middle-class liberals were in the forefront of the attack on wealthy landowners, they soon pounced on huge wealth regardless of its source. Since the late nineteenth century, the issue of land ownership has faded; progressive taxation of all income and wealth, which differ from each other (land ownership, Lindert points out, "may be a poor guide to overall economic inequality"), became the target. The conspicuous feature of land ownership in London, which held a fifth of the nation's real estate value, is the extent of how many were landless. By the end of that century, says Barbara Daniels, three times more people lived in

Great Britain than they did at its beginning—largely because of the industrial revolution, one result of which was that people, skilled and unskilled, flocked into cities and towns to seek employment. Because men had barely enough for themselves and their families to live on when they had work, they had no savings to fall back on when they were laid off or could not find jobs. "All these problems were magnified in London where the population grew at a record rate. Large houses were turned into flats and tenements and the landlords who owned them were not concerned about the upkeep or the condition of these dwellings." In some houses, thirty or more people could live in one room. Those who could not afford their rents themselves rented space in their room to one or more lodgers for a few pence a day. With excessive wealth and extreme poverty so close to each other, slums and rookeries were a stone's throw from the elegant houses of the rich.[10]

And in Gilded Age 2.0? "Only the Rich Could Love This Economic Recovery" is the title of a 2021 *New York Times* article on the United States by Karen Petrou. When the year began, "the richest 1% of Americans held 32% of the nation's wealth, its highest level since these records began in 1989. The bottom 50%, meanwhile, held just 2% of the nation's wealth." Worse still, this record follows a year of "huge economic stimulus and more than a decade of rock-bottom interest rates." Whom did they actually help? The lower 50 percent reaped $700 billion. "But this is a pittance compared with the mammoth gains for the ever fewer who are even richer: in the same period, the richest 1 percent gained $10 trillion." One major cause is tax policies, which for decades have favored wealthy individuals and corporations. The U.S. Federal Reserve System's approach is based on what she accurately calls "trickle-down expectations," advocated by Ronald Reagan in the eighties and adopted in the early 2000s. "In truth," she adds, "this policy works only for the wealthy." In truth, too, the Federal Reserve's low interest rates hurt those who put their savings in banks rather than in the stock market. Assuming ordinary people had $10,000 in spare cash, if they invested it in a bank in 2007, for example, with interest compounded at half of 1 percent, its value in June 2021 would be $12,336; accounting for inflation, $9529, which we should note is less than the original investment. If, by contrast they invested $10,000 in the stock market, its June 2021 rise would be 201 percent, its value $30,100; after inflation, $23,250. The result, she concludes in a well-chosen phrase, is "wealth without prosperity." As for the U.K., Graham Snowden predicted, also this year,

"Wage disparity between the UK's top earners and the rest of the working population will soon return to the levels of the Victorian era unless action is taken to curb executive pay, a new report by the high pay commission claims." According to this commission, "if current trends continue, the top 0.1% of UK earners will see their pay rise from 5% to an estimated 14% of national income by 2030, a level not previously seen in the UK since the start of the 20th century." Its chair, Deborah Hargreaves, said the report showed that "the pay gap between the corporate elite and the general public was widening beyond control." The Institute for Fiscal Studies confirmed that "income among the top 1–2% of earners grew much faster than for the majority of workers during the Labour government years, a factor the report blames for an increase in social inequality since 1997." Making matters worse is the further unequal distribution of wealth in the United States by race, especially between White and Black—worse because less wealth means employment and mortgage discrimination, thus fewer home owners, less tax benefits and savings, and fewer chances for upward mobility in the present and fewer opportunities to save and build wealth to pass to future generations. The cycle of wealth inequality increases among the lower and middle classes, and increases further among Blacks and other people of color.[11]

To go back to Shaw's time, let us relate income disparity to *Major Barbara*, another aspect of which I treated earlier.[12] For a long time after Jane Austen's nineteenth-century novels were written, audiences recognized their allusions to money—and this is also true of Shaw's plays—less so now, partly because inflation was insignificant until World War I. As Thomas Piketty states, "monetary markers were extremely stable." For quite a while readers and spectators pretty much knew what the figures meant. Monetary signifiers are prominent in *Major Barbara*, which treats them among lower and upper classes. "I am a Millionaire. That is my religion," says Undershaft. Even today we know what he means. He is one of "the 1 percent," a term from the title of a 2006 documentary film directed by Jamie Johnson, which characterizes people earning far above what the other 99 percent do. As there is no single "correct" way to assess monetary value years later, for many contexts determine its worth, I use the Bank of England Inflation Calculator, which employs an average inflation rate to give a 1905 pound's 2020 value as £124, as sufficiently reliable. Simple arithmetic gives equivalents in 1905 U.S. dollars (just multiply by five), but as I type these words in late April 2022 £1 costs less: $1.24. By definition, a British millionaire in 1905 had, at minimum,

£1,000,000. Inflation would make it worth about £125 million today, or about $150 million (to prevent a reader's eyes from glazing over, I round figures up or down, with such phrases as "about" and "over"). Among the lowest class characters, Snobby Price tells Rummy that his wages are thirty-eight shillings a week when he can get it, which was just under £2; adjusted for inflation, about £250 today ($310, which is about the U.S. federal minimum wage, $7.25 an hour). In the 1941 movie version Snobby says his salary would be 3 pounds, 10 shillings a week—roughly twice that of 1905 ($180, still low). It is unsurprising that Mrs. Baines is thrilled by Bodger's offer to give the Army £5000 if five others would contribute £1000 each to make the total £10,000 and is ecstatic when Undershaft offers to match the £50,000 singlehandedly (the figures are unchanged in the movie version). Today the joint offer would be over half a million pounds (roughly $630,000)—a striking contrast to what Barbara raises at street meetings. Higher up the economic scale, Lady Britomart's father, whom she calls poor (his income is hardly £7000 per annum) in relation to Undershaft, who she tells her son in Act 1 is rolling in money. Adjusted for inflation, her father's income would be £900,000 (close to $1¼ million) today. Shaw does not reveal how much Undershaft gives his estranged wife, but it is enough for her to maintain a house—with "more than a necessary minimum of domestic servants" (in Piketty's phrase about Austen's works), including a butler—in fashionable Wilton Crescent, in London's Belgravia district, where Old Bill Buoyant the Billionaire, in Shaw's *Buoyant Billions*, resides. Today the Singapore and Luxembourg embassies are on that quiet street, two blocks away from noisy Knightsbridge. As for Cusins's salary, Undershaft offers to start this neophyte in business at £1000 a year—still the mark of "a significant divide" (Piketty's term) in 1905 and 25 percent more than Lomax receives. Rejecting it, he demands £2500 a year for two years, after which he will leave if he is a failure, but if he is successful he wants an additional £5000 to bring the two-year salary to £5000 a year. For year three he calls for 10 percent of the profits. Undershaft's counterproposal is half and they settle on three-fifths. They agree on what in today's inflated figures would total over £600,000 a year (more than $800,000) and possibly six percent of the profits in the third year. We still do not know what Undershaft's income or wealth is, but if he is not in the top 0.1 percent, he is surely in the top 1 percent. Cusins's skillful bargaining about his salary, which pleases Undershaft, suggests that as head of the firm his eventual income bracket will be no lower than his adoptive father's.

In the title of this book, "Shaw" is the last word. Let me end the book by giving him, rather than any of his characters, the last word. Particularly in view of the discussions of capitalism, enlightened capitalism, nationalization, and socialism in Chapters 7 and 8, I quote from the sixth and last of his lectures at the end of 1914 (in which he refers to the Colorado strike and the Dublin lockout, both explored in Chapter 4), which he delivered at London's 2000-seat Kingsway Hall, on the redistribution of income. You, he told the audience, are in a stage of society "which is dying out and which is not staying. The conditions of society you are in is extraordinarily unstaying. When you come to those terrible conflicts such as the fight between Larkin, in [the 1913] Dublin [Lockout], and the citizens generally, and the [1913–1914 mining] war in Colorado," you must consider whether to continue this "state of things or whether there shall be interposition of the State itself, of the whole community, to take the matter out of the hands of the strike leaders and capitalists, and to impose a common ideal for the whole community."[13] The present conditions are not permanent or even temporary solutions. To repeat his word, they are "unstaying." What may come next is up to his listeners and readers, and those whom they may influence.

Notes

1. John Jewkes, "The Nationalization of Industry," *University of Chicago Law Review*, 20.4 (Summer 1953): 616, 620, 622–24, https://core.ac.uk/download/pdf/234131715.pdf; Tejvan Pettinger, "Arguments for Nationalisation," *Economics Help*, 28 October 2019, https://www.economicshelp.org/macroeconomics/privatisation/nationalisation/.
2. Nathan Osafao Omane, "The Effects of Nationalisation on the British Coal Industry," *Economics*, 27 April 2021, https://etonomics.com/2021/04/27/the-effects-of-nationalisation-on-the-british-coal-industry/.
3. D.W. Dixon-Hardyand and I.G. Ediz, "The U.K. Coal Industry Since Privatisation in 1995," *17th International Mining Congress and Exhibition of Turkey*, 2001, pp. 589–94, https://www.maden.org.tr/resimler/ekler/0f800c92d191d73_ek.pdf.
4. John Jewkes, "The Nationalization of Industry," *University of Chicago Law Review*, 20.4 (Summer 1953): 625; Elizabeth Tandy Shermer, "The Right to Work Really Means the Right to Work for Less," *Washington Post*, 24 April 2018, https://www.washingtonpost.com/news/made-by-history/wp/2018/04/24/the-right-to-work-really-means-the-right-to-work-for-less/.

5. James G. Moher, "The Osborne Judgement of 1909: Trade Union Funding of Political Parties in Historical Perspective," *History & Policy*, 2 December 2009, https://www.historyandpolicy.org/policy-papers/papers/the-osborne-judgement-of-1909-trade-union-funding-of-political-parties-in-h; "1913 Trade Union Act," *Spartacus Educational*, https://spartacus-educational.com/Ltrade13.htm; "1927 Trade Disputes Act," *Spartacus Educational*, https://spartacus-educational.com/Ltrade27.htm.
6. "Ronald Reagan Testifies Before HUAC (1947)," *Alpha History*, https://alphahistory.com/coldwar/ronald-reagan-testifies-huac-1947/; B.P. Perry, "How Thatcher Broke the Miners' Strike But at What Cost?" *History*, https://www.history.co.uk/article/how-thatcher-broke-the-miners-strike-but-at-what-cost; Ric, "Did Thatcher Break the Trade Unions?" *Flip Chart Fairy Tales*, 8 April 2013, https://flipchartfairytales.wordpress.com/2013/04/08/did-thatcher-break-the-trade-unions/; Donald MacIntyre, "How the Miners' Strike of 1984–85 Changed Britain Forever," *New Statesman*, 16 June 2015, https://www.newstatesman.com/politics/2014/06/how-miners-strike-1984-85-changed-britain-ever; Nicholas Jones, "Viewpoints: How Did Margaret Thatcher Change Britain?" *BBC News*, 10 April 2013, https://www.bbc.com/news/uk-politics-22076774.
7. Brian Craig, "Reagan vs. Air Traffic Controllers," UVA Miller Center, https://millercenter.org/reagan-vs-air-traffic-controllers; Todd Johnson, "Ronald Reagan and the PATCO Strike: Broken Promises and a Broken Union," *The History Rat*, https://historyrat.wordpress.com/2012/10/14/reagan-and-the-patco-strike-broken-promises/; "Details on State Right-to-Work Laws," *FindLaw*, 20 June 2016, https://statelaws.findlaw.com/employment-laws/details-on-state-right-to-work-laws.html; Ronald V. Sires, "The Repeal of the Trade Disputes and Trade Unions Act of 1927," *ILR Review* (January 1953), 6.2: 230–32, 237, https://www.jstor.org/stable/2518643?origin=crossref&seq=11#metadata_info_tab_contents.
8. "Four Years of Trump: The Record Speaks For Itself," *News for Working People*, 13 October 2020, https://nwlaborpress.org/2020/10/four-years-of-trump-the-record-speaks-for-itself/; "Anti-Union Actions by the Trump Administration," *Chicago Laborers' District Council*, 12 October 2020, https://www.liunachicago.org/about-us/news/details/2147/anti-union-actions-by-the-trump-administration; "Senator Josh Hawley's Speech at the National Conservative Conference," *Josh Hawley U.S. Senator for Missouri*, https://www.hawley.senate.gov/senator-josh-hawleys-speech-national-conservatism-conference.
9. John Jewkes, "The Nationalization of Industry," *University of Chicago Law Review*, 20.4 (Summer 1953): 645.

10. Peter H. Lindert, "Who Owned Victorian England? The Debate Over Landed Wealth and Inequality," *Agricultural History* (Autumn, 1987), 61.4: 25–26, 35, https://shibbolethsp.jstor.org/start?entityID=urn%3Amace%3Aincommon%3Avt.edu&dest=https://www.jstor.org/stable/3743895&site=jstor; Barbara Daniels, "Poverty and Families in the Victorian Era," *Hidden Lives Revealed*, March 2003, https://www.hiddenlives.org.uk/articles/poverty.html.
11. Karen Petrou, "Only the Rich Could Love This Economic Recovery," *New York Times*, 12 July 2021, https://www.nytimes.com/interactive/2021/07/12/opinion/covid-fed-qe-nequality.html; Graham Snowden, "Pay Gap Widening to Victorian Levels," *The Guardian*, 16 May 2011, https://www.theguardian.com/business/2011/may/16/high-pay-commission-wage-disparity; Angela Hanks, Danyelle Solomon, and Christian E. Weller, "Systematic Inequality: How America's Structural Racism Helped Create the Black-White Wealth Gap," *Center for American Progress*, 21 February 2018, https://www.americanprogress.org/issues/race/reports/2018/02/21/447051/systematic-inequality/.
12. This paragraph draws on the article Bernard F. Dukore, "How Much? Understanding Money in *Major Barbara*," *SHAW: The Journal of Bernard Shaw Studies*, 36.1 (2016): 73–81, which is largely based on the important book by Thomas Piketty, *Capital in the Twenty-First Century*, trans. Arthur Goldhammer (Cambridge, MA: Harvard University Press, 2014).
13. Bernard Shaw, "Who Will Do the Drudgery in a Socialistic Community," *New York American*, 6 January 1915: reprinted in "Six Fabian Lectures on Redistribution of Income," ed. Peter Gahan, *SHAW: The Annual of Bernard Shaw Studies: Shaw and Money*, ed. Audrey McNamara and Nelson O'Ceallaigh Ritschel, 36.1 (2016): 10–52.

Index

B. F. Dukore, *Unions, Strikes, Shaw*,
Bernard Shaw and His Contemporaries,
https://doi.org/10.1007/978-3-030-99131-9

The manufacturer's authorised representative in the EU is Springer Nature Customer Service Centre GmbH, Europaplatz 3, 69115 Heidelberg, Germany. If you have any concerns regarding our products, please contact ProductSafety@springernature.com

Printed and bound by CPI Group (UK) Ltd, Croydon, CR0 4YY
30/09/2026
02225475-0004